BE

Believing Is Seeing

PETER GAMMONS

KINGSWAY PUBLICATIONS
EASTBOURNE

First published 1987

ISBN 0 86065 405 2

Front cover: Art Directors Photolibrary–London

Printed in Great Britain for
KINGSWAY PUBLICATIONS LTD
Lottbridge Drove, Eastbourne, E. Sussex BN23 6NT by
Cox & Wyman Ltd, Reading
Typeset by Nuprint Services Ltd, Harpenden, Herts AL5 4SE

Contents

Acknowledgements

My thanks go to Jean Liddicoate and Andrea Hughes, who between them spent numerous hours typing this manuscript. Also to Derek Minto, Dave Evans, Pat Darwood and others for their editorial assistance.

Introduction

When Jesus said, 'Whatever you ask in my name, that I will do, that the Father may be glorified in the Son' (John 14:13), he meant it.

GOD INTENDS OUR PRAYERS TO BE ANSWERED

So many Christians' lives are stale, religious and powerless, far removed from the 'life more abundant' which Jesus said that he had come to bring us (John 10:10). The idea that it is extremely difficult to get God to answer prayer, let alone 'all' prayer, is one of the lies with which Satan has fooled the church for too long. It is a lie that God wants to destroy.

As we look at Jesus' life and the lives of his disciples, one of the things which stands out is that miracles were a normal part of life. *Their lives were naturally supernatural.* Why should we settle for anything less? Jesus said of believers that we would do greater things than he did because he was going to the Father (John 14:12). Yet so many Christians neither expect nor see the miraculous power of God in their lives.

I trust that you will find this a balanced and helpful

volume. I have sought in part one to emphasize the positive aspects of faith, and have also considered such important subjects as how to react when our faith is tried or when God does not answer our prayer the way we had hoped he would. It is my desire that as a result of reading this many will meet with the Lord and be healed. In part two I have considered in more depth some of the major hindrances to answered prayer, basing the study around the Lord's Prayer. In part three I have looked at some of the areas into which we can move by faith.

It is my hope that this book will become a frequent source of inspiration and encouragement to you, rather than something you read only once. More importantly, may it turn you afresh, with renewed confidence, to the immutable Word of God and enlarge your vision of his greatness and power.

Peter Gammons

PART ONE

God Intends Your Prayers to Be Answered

1

It's Him-Possible

The Bible is an exciting account of God's dealings with men and women like you and me. We need to destroy the idea that there was something weird or unnatural about the people in the Bible. They were mostly ordinary people who faced every situation in life with faith. So many Christians, when reading the biblical accounts of the things God did through the lives of such men as Abraham, Moses, Elijah and Elisha, read them as though they were a 'Superman' story. They sigh wistfully, thinking, 'Wasn't it wonderful? Weren't they marvellous people? I could never be like them.' God does not want us to read the Bible in that way. He wants us to let our faith rise, to believe that he can do similar things in our lives! Elijah was 'a man with a nature like ours' (James 5:17). The only great thing about him was the God he served! And we have the same God.

God took ordinary people, like fishermen, tax collectors and shepherds and did extra-ordinary things through their lives. He has chosen 'the foolish things of the world to put to shame the wise… that no flesh should glory in his presence' (1 Corinthians 1:27, 29).

The Bible does not glamourise their life stories, but reveals many of their failings. However, despite their failures, they were people who discovered what it is to live by faith. They learned something of the greatness and the power of God.

In Hebrews 11 we find a tremendous account of God's miraculous movings in response to faith. We hear of a barren elderly woman bearing a child; the seemingly impenetrable walls of Jericho falling; the dead being raised and the Red Sea crossed, by faith. Our God has not changed. The biblical accounts are not fairy tales. They really happened and miracles are still taking place today.

A God of miracles

A young girl who had recently been converted was reading the account of Israel's miraculous crossing of the Red Sea (Exodus 14) during one of her Religious Education lessons at school. Excitement began to well up inside her until, unable to contain her joy any longer, she shouted out, 'Hallelujah!'

Her stunned teacher said, 'Why did you just shout out "Hallelujah"?'

The girl replied, 'Isn't it wonderful how God parted the Red Sea, so that the children of Israel could cross on dry land?'

Her sceptical teacher responded, 'Well, it wasn't actually the Red Sea they crossed. Many theologians believe that it was the "Reed Sea", which is only four inches deep. So you see it wasn't a miracle really.'

The girl quietly continued to read the passage and then let out another 'Hallelujah!'

The teacher, more surprised than ever, asked,

'What is it now?'

The girl eagerly replied, 'The whole of the Egyptian army was drowned in four inches of water!'

Whichever way you look at it, it was a miracle! Our God is a miracle working God.

When the angel was informing Mary that she had been chosen to be the mother of God's Son, even though she was a virgin, he said, '*With God nothing will be impossible*' (Luke 1:37). Do we really believe that? Sometimes we are faced with situations in life where a solution seems out of the question. It seems as though things have gone too far even for God to intervene. However, we need to realize that even though it might look impossible, it is 'him-possible'. All things are possible with him. God specializes in solving seemingly impossible situations. *When all around you seems hopeless, you can confess in faith, 'The situation looks totally him-possible.'*

With God, there is no such thing as an easy or difficult miracle. Healing a cancer is no more difficult than healing a headache. Circumstances do not dictate to God. He is all-powerful!

Divine co-operation

However, the Scriptures do not only teach that 'with God nothing will be impossible'; Jesus said of the believer, 'All things are possible *to him who believes*' (Mark 9:23). Most Christians have no problem with the statement that nothing is impossible with God, even though for many it remains mere theory that fails to affect their lives. But few really believe that nothing is impossible for us, if we only can believe. Yet this is what Jesus said. *Faith is the hand which reaches into the unseen and brings it into the seen.* Faith reaches into God's unlimited supply and brings it down to meet the needs we have in our lives. Faith simply takes God at his word. It believes that he will do the things which he says he will do.

God did not make thousands of promises in his word merely to fill up the pages. He was not sitting in heaven thinking of things to put in the Bible to pad it out! When God gave us the promises in his word, he did so because he intends to fulfil them. He wants us to experience the healing, provision, new life and the freedom that he has provided. But he calls us to reach out by faith to receive them: that is God going into partnership with man. Nothing is impossible with God and he says, 'Now by faith, if you can believe, nothing will be impossible for you.' Nothing will be beyond the reach of your faith.

The Bible describes us as *God's fellow workers*. We read that the disciples went out, 'the Lord working *with* them and confirming the word through the accompanying signs' (Mark 16:20). They were not merely God's servants, God worked with them. Do you realize you are God's fellow worker? You are not called just to work for God but to work with him.

Of course, God could do anything without our co-operation if he so desired. He is sovereign. However, in his sovereignty, he has chosen to work with us. In his grace and mercy, he has allowed us to have a part in the things which he is doing. We are far more than spectators. You've probably heard of the Christian who one day, eager to witness to his unconverted neighbour, decided to talk about the beauty of creation. His opening line was, 'Hasn't God given you a beautiful garden?' However, he was stunned by his neighbours quick reply. 'Yes, but you should have seen it five years ago when God had it all to himself!' It was true that God had given the man a beautiful garden; nevertheless, the man made a valid point that it had involved co-operation. The idea that things will happen all the same, whether we pray or not, is misguided and unscriptural. It is like saying, 'Why bother washing your hands? If God wants them clean, they will come clean.'

In Ezekiel, we read the sad account of how God looked for someone to 'stand in the gap' between himself and his people, that he might not destroy them for their wickedness, but could not find anyone (Ezekiel 22:30).

When Gideon questioned why God was not moving on Israel's behalf in a miraculous way, as he had done in the past, God pointed out that Gideon had forgotten something. Yes, he had led them out of Egypt and parted the Red Sea, but he had used Moses to accomplish his purposes. For God has chosen to work in partnership with men. 'And Gideon,' said God, 'guess who I'm going to use next... ?'

Notice how men were involved in Jesus' miracles, whether it was bringing the paralytic to him, distributing the food to the hungry multitude, removing the stone from Lazarus' tomb, or collecting the 'unconverted' water and then presenting it, blessed by Jesus, to the wedding host.

Such responses were faith in action. The human/divine partnership.

Anything!

There are many things that, unles we do them or receive them by faith, will not be done. As we have seen, the Bible does not present us with a picture of some sovereign God doing whatever he pleases, whenever he pleases. Rather he is a sovereign God, who has called us into partnership with himself, one who has chosen to do extraordinary things through the lives of ordinary people. Listen to some of Jesus' promises:

> *Whatever* you ask in my name, that *I will do*, that the Father may be glorified in the Son (John 14:13).
> If you ask *anything* in my name, *I will do it* (John 14:14).
> If you abide in me, and my words abide in you, you will ask what you *desire*, and it shall be done for you (John 15:7).
> Most assuredly, I say to you, *whatever* you ask the Father in my name he *will* give you (John 16:23).
> Until now you have asked nothing in my name. Ask, and *you will receive*, that your joy may be full (John 16:24).
> Again I say to you that if two of you agree on earth concerning *anything* that they ask, it will be done for them by my Father in heaven (Matthew 18:19).
> And all things, *whatever* you ask in prayer, believing, you *will* receive (Matthew 21:22).
> Therefore, I say to you, *whatever* things you ask when you pray, believe that you receive them, and you *will* have them (Mark 11:24).

Notice how Jesus freely uses such terms as 'whatever' and 'anything you ask'. He does not say God 'might' or 'could' answer our prayers or that there is a 'vague possibility'. Rather, he positively affirms, 'It will be done'; 'It shall be done.'

Notice, too, to whom these promises are addressed:

'*you*'! 'Ask, and you *will* receive, that your joy may be full' (John 16:24). You are important to God. He wants to do more for you than just answer the occasional prayer.

God is not moody!

We need to see that God is not our problem when it comes to answered prayer. Prayer is not trying to twist God's arm to do things against his will. We do not come to a reluctant God, who does not want to bless us or to answer our prayers. God is not moody. It is the devil who wants us to believe that. God says, 'You do not have because you do not ask' (James 4:2). In the back of many Christians' minds there is the sneaking suspicion that prayer is a waste of time. We claim that we do not have time to pray, but we find time to do the things which we really want to do. Many Christians seem to have the idea that God puts everyone's name in a hat and then pulls out names at random, to discover those he will bless that night, like some Grand Draw. Everyone waits on the edge of his chair, while the 'winner' is called. Then as everyone stands to leave, the announcement is made, 'Come next week to see if your needs will be met.' Though this may sound ridiculous, it is a concept many really subscribe to. 'Que sera sera; whatever will be, will be.' Fatalism is an ungodly and anti-biblical concept. By faith we have the ability to change, affect and initiate events. It is by faith that we reach out and receive miracles. God does not call us to sit back passively waiting to discover his will in the outcome of events.

Hannah prayed while she was barren and received a child. Elijah prayed and fire fell from heaven, demonstrating God's superiority over Baal. The early church prayed and Peter was miraculously delivered from jail, where he had been awaiting execution. Hezekiah prayed when he was dying and the Lord added fifteen more years to his life. 'The effective, fervent prayer of a righteous man avails much. Elijah was a man with a nature like ours, and he prayed earnestly that it would not rain; and it did not rain on the land for three years and six months. And he prayed again, and the heaven gave rain, and the earth produced its fruit' (James 5:16b–18).

Heaven's currency

Faith is the currency of heaven. Jesus said, 'If you can believe, all things are possible to him who believes' (Mark 9:23).

'Whatever things you ask when you pray, believe that you receive them' (Mark 11:24). Reception of the answers to our prayers is conditional upon our having faith for them.

If you look at the miracles of Jesus, you will see that faith was the common denominator. He often said such things as, 'According to your faith let it be to you' (Matthew 9:29). 'Do you believe I am able to do this?' (Matthew 9:28). 'Your faith has made you well' (Matthew 9:22). Faith is far more than an intellectual believing that what God says is true. Faith takes God at his word: 'Lord, I believe you will do it because you have promised.' True faith is not passive, it brings results.

When Jesus prayed, or simply spoke the word of faith, things happened. He got results. The dead were raised. The sick were healed. Needs were met. The bound were set free. Water was turned into wine. Five thousand unexpected dinner guests were fed. The tax bill was paid. Listen to Jesus' words as he stood praying outside Lazarus' tomb: 'Father, I thank you that you have heard me. And I know that you always hear me, but because of the people who are standing by I say this, that they may believe that you sent me' (John 11:41–42). In other words, he was saying, 'Anything I ask will be done.' Then he simply spoke the words, 'Lazarus, come forth!' and the dead man was raised back to life again (John 11:43–44). You might say, 'Well, that was Jesus. We can't expect that kind of miracle today, can we?' But Jesus said, 'He who believes in me, the works that I do he will do also; and greater works than these he will do, because I go to my Father' (John 14:12).

Maybe you are sick. Maybe there are financial problems. Maybe you are concerned for an unsaved friend or relative. Do you believe that the situation is him-possible? Although God does not want us to be selfish, and sometimes wrong attitudes do rob us of blessings, as we will be considering later, he does still want to meet our needs and to give us the desires of our hearts.

Typewriters, duplicators and swimming pools

One Christmas I was preaching at a small chapel near my home. I had only been saved a couple of years and was still in secular employment, though I was leading a small team who ministered in chapels around East Anglia. I was largely unknown and rarely received my petrol expenses on trips, let alone any love gifts. That Sunday I was speaking at a little chapel which had about twelve people in the congregation. It was a typical, hour long service, with a twenty minute message. As I was quietly sitting there, having just announced that we would have a time of silent prayer, I felt God say to me, 'Peter, what would you like for Christmas?'

I thought for a moment and said, 'Lord, I'd like a swimming pool. You know, one of those family-sized ones, to put in the garden. And for the ministry, we need a typewriter and we also need a duplicator, to produce the chorus sheets and follow up letters. Okay?'

Nobody heard me pray and no one had any idea of the desires of my heart, apart from the Lord. At the end of the service, I went down and was shaking hands with people at the door as they left. It came to the last three people and as a lady went to leave, she turned back and said, 'Would you like a typewriter?'

I replied, 'Pardon?'

She repeated, 'Would you like a typewriter? I used to be a secretary, but I've not used my typewriter for years. Maybe you could use it?'

I said, 'That's tremendous! I've been praying that the Lord would provide one.'

She said, 'You can come and collect it now if you like.'

Her son, who was with her, said, 'Would you like a duplicator as well?' He continued, 'I bought a duplicator to use in the church, but we never duplicate anything, so if you could use it, you may as well have it.'

I said, 'Thank you very much,' and they left. I thought, 'Lord, that's great. Two out of three.' (The 'spiritual' ones!)

I finally said goodbye to the church secretary and

just as I was walking out the door, he said, 'By the way, you don't want a swimming pool, do you?'

Slightly stunned at the speed at which my prayers were being answered, I said 'Why?'

He replied, 'Well, we bought a family-sized one to use as a baptistry, but we've only used it twice. It takes so long to fill and empty it that it's easier to borrow a neighbouring church's baptistry. So if you want it, you can have it.'

I do not want to give the impression that all prayer is answered as immediately as on this occasion. As we will consider in some depth later, it is 'by faith and patience' that we inherit God's promise. Nevertheless, that day I left with a typewriter, a duplicator, a swimming pool and a renewed awareness of God's love for me and the power there is in the prayer of faith.

2

That Settles It

One night, when faith was really high during one of our camp meetings, the guest speaker announced, 'All childless couples who believe God can give you a child, stand to your feet.'

Many young couples began to stand, but there was one rather elderly gentleman, sitting on the front row, who was rather deaf, and thought he had said, 'All those who believe God, stand to your feet.' So, amidst those young couples, this elderly man stood to his feet.

His wife grabbed his arm and dragged him down, shouting in his ear, 'He said, those who believe God can give them a child, not those who believe God.'

The very embarrassed man said, 'Oh.'

I was in hysterics, when suddenly God quietly spoke to me and said, 'Don't you believe I could do it?' I was instantly struck afresh with amazement at the God we serve.

Just think of the odds against Abraham and Sarah having a child! Abraham was ninety-nine years old and Sarah at ninety was well past the menopause, but God promised them a child. Listen to God's promises: 'Look now towards heaven, and count the stars if you are able to number them.... So shall your descendants be' (Genesis 15:5). 'My covenant I will establish with Isaac, whom Sarah shall bear to you at this set time next year' (Genesis 17:21). To the natural mind, such a promise is both ridiculous and impossible. But it is 'him-possible'.

When he promised Abraham a child, God added, 'Is anything too hard for the Lord?' (Genesis 18:14). I want to ask you that same question. Is anything too hard for the Lord? Is meeting your need too hard for the Lord? There is no problem that is bigger than God!

Often after a meeting, people will say, 'I didn't come forward for prayer because there are people far worse off than I am.' This may sound noble but in reality it is an insult to the Lord. It is implying that if we draw on God's power to meet our little problems, there will not be enough left for the big ones. We need to see that God is almighty, he has enough power to deal with all our little problems and all the big ones.

Un-common sense

The Bible tells us that, 'The natural man does not receive the things of the Spirit of God, for they are foolishness to him; nor can he know them, because they are spiritually discerned' (1 Corinthians 2:14). To the natural mind, the possibility of Abraham and Sarah having a child was ridiculous. Sadly many Christians read God's word sceptically, sifting it through the natural mind. How often have you heard Christians say, 'But God has given us common sense.' Who wants anything common? We are part of a new kingdom! God wants totally to renew our thinking. True, God has given us 'sense', he has made us rational beings. But the Bible tells us that 'the just shall live by faith' (Romans 1:17)—not by common sense.

Often, God's promises defy common sense. God has given certain laws, such as the law of gravity. But he easily can override them to fulfil his purposes. Common sense does not get out of a boat and walk on water! Common sense says, 'I'm staying in the boat where it's safe,' and misses out on a miracle. Common sense does not try feeding over five thousand people with a little boy's lunch! Common sense does not expect a couple of senior, senior citizens to have a child! When your common sense contradicts God's word, what do you believe? Do you accept the information your common sense gives you or do you believe God and his word? Abraham and Sarah chose to believe God.

GOD SAID IT, THAT SETTLES IT!

Paul says of Abraham: 'Not being weak in faith, he did not consider [by common sense] his own body, already dead (since he was about a hundred years old), and the deadness of Sarah's womb. He did not waver at *the promise of God* through unbelief, but was strengthened in faith, giving glory to God, and being fully convinced that *what he had promised* he was also able to perform' (Romans 4:19–21). Abraham chose not to believe his common sense nor to believe his circumstances; he chose to believe God!

Faith's foundation

True faith is founded on God's word. A vital condition for receiving our inheritance and the fulfilment of his promises is that we stand on God's promises. How many times have you heard someone say, 'I *believe*'? However, the Bible tells us that even the devil believes and trembles (James 2:19). Satan is totally convinced that God is almighty and that his word is true! What do you believe? Believing is far more than just an intellectual understanding or agreeing with a set of doctrinal statements.

The Greek word for 'believe' is *pisteuo,* which means, 'to be persuaded of and hence to place confidence in, to trust, to rely upon'. The Greek word for 'faith' is *pistis*, which means 'a firm persuasion, a conviction based on hearing'. These are far removed from the attitude, 'Well, I hope God will answer my prayer. I hope he will heal me.' That is not a firm persuasion; that is not 'a conviction based on hearing'. True believing says, 'God said it, that settles it.'

The word of God is the will of God

If you want to know what God's will is—read it. We call the two sections of the Bible the Old Testament and the New Testament and that is exactly what the Bible is: God's 'last will and testament'. Before someone dies he leaves a will to let his heirs know what their inheritance is. Because Jesus had died, we now have an inheritance. If you want to know what it is, read the will!

I recently read in the papers about a lady who died without making a will, leaving £670,000 which she had accumulated by playing the stock market. An eighteen month search had failed to find any blood relatives. Somewhere there were potentially rich relatives, but they did not know that the fortune was theirs. In the same way, so many Christians live spiritually impoverished lives because they do not realize the inheritance of forgiveness, health and provision which is theirs because Christ died. As Christians, we are rich! God has made multitudes of promises to us. Yet so often we do not experience them because we have not read the will.

God's word is immutable. Jesus said, 'Heaven and earth will pass away, but my words will by no means pass away' (Matthew 24:35).

'All the promises of God in him are "Yes," and in him "Amen," to the glory of God' (2 Corinthians 1:20). *Before we even claim God's promises, he has already said 'Yes'*. All the promises are 'Yes' and 'Amen' (so be it)—'to the glory of God'. God's reputation is at stake if he does not keep his word.

> God is not a man, that he should lie,
> Nor a son of man,
> that he should repent.
> Has he said, and will he not do it?
> Or has he spoken,
> and will he not make it good?
>
> Numbers 23:19

For example, imagine I said to you, 'Would you like to come for a meal with me tomorrow evening? I'll see you at seven and we'll go to the Ritz.' However, when you turn up at seven o'clock in your best clothes, I arrive wearing a pair of jeans and a tee shirt.

Surprised at my appearance, you say, 'Do you normally go to the Ritz dressed like that?'

I reply sheepishly, 'Well, talking of the Ritz, er, I know that I promised to take you to the Ritz. Well, the truth is, I can't afford to take you there, but I know a lovely fish and chip shop down the road that does a great cod and chips.'

My reputation would now be at stake! The next time I invited you to go to the Ritz, you would probably turn up in jeans and a tee shirt! If I were to invite someone else for a meal, you would probably take them aside and warn them, 'You think you're going to the Ritz. Well, I wouldn't build up your hopes; he told me that he'd take me there, but he never actually did. Do you like fish and chips?'

'All the promises of God are "Yes," and "Amen," *to the glory of God.*'

God is not afraid to commit himself. He has committed himself to his word. God is not unscriptural! If he said it, that settles it. God cannot lie (Titus 1:2 and Numbers 23:19). So, how do we discover God's will on any given subject? Through the Bible. Faith is not a shot in the dark. It is not praying, 'If it be thy will', and waiting to discover whether it is God's will by the results. Faith has discovered from God's word what his will is and stands firm, despite contradicting circumstances.

In many, though not all, situations, I believe that we do not see the desired results because we do not pray in faith, rather than because it was not God's will. When Jesus went to Nazareth, he could do no mighty miracles there because of their unbelief. It was his will to do miracles, but their unbelief hindered him (Mark 6:1–6).

If it be thy will?

Many Christians pray, 'If it be thy will', and think that they are thereby being humble or submissive. But usually, rather than indicating humility or submission, it shows ignorance about the word of God. It can also be a way of making unbelief sound spiritual. Unbelief will never bring the desired results. Faith has discovered what God's will is and refuses to be moved. Abraham knew what God's will was and so he stood on his promises, refusing to be put off by any information his body, age or circumstances might give him. If we are going to pray in faith, we need first of all to know God's will on that particular subject. Faith is more than hoping, it is a 'certainty'; a 'conviction that is based on hearing', hearing God's word.

Substance and evidence

'Faith is the substance of things hoped for, the evidence of things not seen' (Hebrews 11:1).

Faith has substance. It is real, graspable. It is not airy-fairy, nor is it wishful thinking. It holds on to the word of God, saying, 'Lord, I believe you. You said you would do it, so I believe it.' It stands firm knowing that God has heard, and that the request is going to be granted, even before there is physical evidence.

Hearing God's word

James tell us to ask in faith, 'with no doubting, for he who doubts is like a wave of the sea driven and tossed by the wind. For let not that man suppose that he will receive anything from the Lord; he is a double minded man, unstable in all his ways' (James 1:6–8).

There is no 'if' in the prayer of faith. The world's philosophy is 'Seeing is believing'—'If I cannot see the evidence with my own eyes, I will not believe it.' But, for the Christian, 'believing is seeing'. We first need to believe if we are to receive.

> If you can *believe*, all things are possible to him who *believes* (Mark 9:23).
> Whatever things you ask when you pray, *believe* that you receive them, and you will have them (Mark 11:24).
> All things, whatever you ask in prayer, *believing*, you will receive (Matthew 21:22).

Although God often gives non-Christians visible evidence of his power before they believe (John 2:23; 6:2), for the Christian, believing usually comes before seeing. It is far easier to pray than to believe. Have you noticed that prayer does not make faith work? Faith makes prayer work. We might be able to pray very eloquently, but it is to our faith that God responds, not to our beautiful speech.

Faith not only has substance; it is also the 'evidence of things not seen' (Hebrews 11:1). The word 'evidence' means 'the absolute proof'. Even before we have any physical evidence of answered prayer, we already have absolute proof. The fact that God said it is sufficient.

The Bible gives two reasons why we miss out on God's blessing. The first is prayerlessness. 'You do not have because you do not ask' (James 4:2). That sums up many Christians. They say, 'God never answers my prayers.' The truth is that they never pray, or, if they do, they pray so vaguely that even if God did answer their prayers, they wouldn't know! The second reason is praying out of his will. 'You ask and do not receive, because you ask amiss' (James 4:3).

We have already seen that God wants to answer

every one of our prayers. He has given us his word, so that we can pray according to his will. God says, 'I want to answer your every prayer, therefore I have given you my word, so that you will know what my will is and can pray according to my will.' If we pray according to the word of God, we cannot pray amiss! 'Now this is the *confidence* that we have in him, that if we ask anything according to his will, he hears us. And if we know that he hears us, *whatever we ask*, we know that we have the petitions that we asked of him' (1 John 5:14–15). God's word comes to correct our ideas. It comes along to renew our thinking and to expel our doubts.

Sand versus rock

The word of God is the only true foundation faith can have. That is why Satan tries to steal the word, saying, 'You don't have to believe that, do you?' The word of God is the only thing we can rely on when opposition comes. To put our trust in anything else is to build on sand. Let us consider some of the other things we can put our faith in.

1. Someone else's opinion

It might be your pastor's opinion or the opinion of a Christian you highly respect. Perhaps they told you God does not heal the sick today. Despite the fact that there are thousands of Christians in England alone who can testify that God miraculously healed them, people still refuse to believe God's word. Are you relying on someone else's opinion or in a doctrine you were once taught? We need to come afresh to God's word and open our hearts to hear what he has to say on the subject. If God said it, that settles it.

2. Our own ideas

Convictions are important, but they must be flexible enough for God to change them through his word. Bigotry is a sin. It is interesting to note that the Greek word for 'heresy' means a 'self-willed opinion'. Many so called 'defenders of the faith' are self-willed in their opinions. We may be entitled to our own opinions, but if our opinions contradict God's word, they are wrong!

The book of Amos asks, 'Can two walk together, unless they are agreed?' (Amos 3:3) If there is a disagreement, God is not going to change his beliefs to agree with ours. We must change to agree with him.

When Elijah told Naaman to dip himself seven times in the Jordan, the great military leader responded, 'Indeed, I said to myself...' (2 Kings 5:11). He had an opinion about how God should heal him. He was entitled to it, but it was wrong! He said, 'Can't we do it another way?' and God said, 'No. Either you do it this way or you don't get the desired results.' He could not have blamed God if he had not been healed.

3. Someone else's experience

This is a dangerous thing to put our faith in, whether the experience was positive or negative. The theory that because another person was healed, you will be healed, is presumption. Although we can be inspired to faith by seeing someone else healed or by hearing their testimony, our faith needs to be in the word of God, not in another person's experience. Alternatively, the attitude, 'I probably won't be healed, because another person was not healed', is mistaken. What does God say?

God's word is the only sure foundation for our faith. It is immutable. There is no 'if' in the prayer of faith. God says it; that settles it.

3

The Source of Faith

'I haven't got enough faith.' How often have you heard someone say that?

'I'd like to see miracles in my life. I want to be healed, but I haven't got enough faith.'

People who say this have misunderstood the source of faith. Faith is not something which unexpectedly falls out of the sky. It comes out of our relationship with the Lord. In any relationship our trust and confidence grow as our relationship grows. Time is needed for a friend to prove himself faithful and reliable.

Jesus is the author and finisher of our faith (Hebrews 12:2). He is the source of the faith we need. *As you look through the biblical accounts you will discover that great men and women of faith were always great men and women with an intimate relationship with God.* The two are inseparable! When you read through accounts of men like Wesley, Finney, Müller and Moody, you will see that they were not only great men of faith but also men who walked closely with the Lord.

Faith is not a rod that we beat God with, to make him do our bidding; or a bell that we pull to summon him, as though he were our servant. I have cringed at times when I have heard Christians pray, ordering God to act. Familiarity must never breed contempt in our relationship with the Lord.

Faith versus emotions

Faith is simply trusting the Lord to keep his word and knowing in your heart that he will do it. Faith is not something that can be forced nor is it something that can be stirred up emotionally. An emotional stirring could be soulish, and not spiritual at all, for our soul consists of the mind, will and emotions. Our emotions could be stirred up by good preaching, but that is not necessarily the same as our faith rising. We can feel great one minute and then feel nothing in particular the next. True faith stands firm when our emotions say nothing or even when our emotions are indicating something negative. I do not always feel emotionally stirred when faith is rising but I have a peaceful confidence within that God has heard and the answer is on the way. Oral Roberts, one of the most well-known faith teaching ministers in the world, made the statement that when you are in faith, 'You know that you know, that you know, that you know', your answer is on the way. *The way to continual faith is through a continual growing, intimate relationship with the Lord. There are no short cuts.* People say, 'I wish I had faith like you, brother.' Well, build your relationship with God, spend time with him; spend time in his word, cultivate a natural twenty-four hour a day friendship with him. That is the way to continued faith.

The Lord and his word are inseparable. Jesus is the Word of God made flesh (John 1:14). Jesus is the Bible translated into visible, human form. Notice how Jesus makes that connection when he says, 'If you abide in *me, and my words* abide in you, you will ask what you desire, and it shall be done for you' (John 15:7).

To 'abide in' means 'to dwell upon' or literally 'to live in'. As we spend time with the Lord, in his word, we discover his will and as we discover what his will is, we can pray in faith, knowing that our prayer will be answered. But it takes time to search the Scriptures to discover God's character, his desires and the promises he makes.

When we are told to pray in his name, that means to pray on his behalf, to pray as he would pray. If we want to know how Jesus would pray when facing sickness, poverty or any other problems, we should read in his word how he reacted when he was on earth, for the word of God is the will of God.

'So then faith comes by hearing, and hearing by the word of God' (Romans 10:17). When God tells us in a situation to have faith, it is not a valid excuse to say, 'But I have not got enough faith.' Lack of faith is our responsibility. If you have not got enough faith go to God's word and get some more, for faith comes by hearing the word of God.

You have the source at hand: open it, read it, get into it! Let faith 'come'. Revelation and faith are inseparable. When God speaks, true faith flows and doubts leave.

The Bible is God's love-letter to us. Can you imagine two people who are in love not wanting to read the love letters which they have sent to each other? You can ask for friends to pray that God will give you a hunger for his word, but better still, pray that you may fall in love with the author. Then you will begin to get excited about the promises he has made to you!

The attitude that a 'quiet time' is 'doing our bit for God', has missed the point. People say, 'I've read my chapter for the day'. God does not want our devotional times to be something boring or legalistic, but enjoyable. We are to 'live in' God's word and then our mind will be renewed so that we think how God thinks. The word of God destroys other people's opinions and kills the seeds of doubt that the devil has sown into our hearts. How we need our minds renewing. Our upbringing, past ideas and past theological teaching shape our thinking, but God says, 'Let my word come and change your thinking. Let my word come and change you, so that you think how I think about situations.' It does not matter what we think about healing. We need to find out what God thinks. It does not matter whether it is something we have 'always believed'. If you have always believed something, maybe it needs reviewing! Chew over God's word. Feed on it. Expect God to speak to you and highlight things from his word.

Out of the total word of God will come specific words to you. Have you noticed that when you read a passage it is as though certain verses have been written in three-dimensional or bold type! Of course, they have not, but they stick out as something specifically written for you at that time.

Logos versus *rhema*

In the Greek there are two words for 'the word of God': *logos* and *rhema*. The *logos* is the total word of God, the whole Bible. It is the inspired word of God. Although God got his different 'secretaries' or 'writers' to write his word down for him, and these men had their own individual styles, God oversaw the work to ensure that no mistakes were made. In the Middle East, there were 'writers' who were employed to write letters for people. The customer would tell the man what he wanted saying and the scribe would put it down in his own words, but then the customer would finally check that what had been written was what he wanted to communicate. That is why the same themes run throughout the Bible, from Genesis to Revelation, even though the Bible was written over many centuries, by different authors. There is a unity about God's word because the writers were basically just God's secretaries.

The *logos* is the total word of God, but the *rhema* is a specific word for a specific situation. *Jesus is the total Word of God, the* Logos, *but out of the Lord came specific words for specific people.* He brought just the word that individual people needed. For example, to the paralytic, Jesus said, 'Arise and walk!' If he had gone up to a blind man and said, 'Arise and walk!' it would not have done a lot of good! One blind man needed to hear, 'Go, wash in the pool of Siloam.' That was a specific word to him. Jesus did not send every blind man to Siloam. Healing is part of our inheritance in Christ; it is God's will for us, but the way he heals us may well be very different with each one of us. For some it might be instantaneous; for others there might be a journey of faith to Siloam.

Jesus came walking on the water and said to Peter, 'Come' (Matthew 14:28–29). That was an invitation to Peter to get out of the boat and walk. In one sense, Peter did not walk on the water; he walked on Jesus' word! He stepped out in faith having received a specific *rhema* word.

When Jesus said to the woman at the well, 'You have had five husbands, and the one whom you now have is not your husband' (John 4:18), that was a specific word to her. It is not the scripture to give everybody!

All of the Bible is unquestionably the word of God, but there are times when God brings that *rhema* word, that living word, which we know is a specific word into our situation. We know that God has spoken. The Bible is like a diamond with many different facets. You can read each passage numerous times and God can bring something new out of it on each occasion. You can read one of your favourite passages which you have read many times and God can still bring something fresh from it, because it is alive. The Bible has been described as 'the book with God in it'.

When Jesus said, 'Man shall not live by bread alone, but by every *word* that proceeds out of the mouth of God' (Matthew 4:4), he chose the Greek word *rhema*. The *rhema*, God's specific word, proceeds from the *logos*, the total word of God.

Faith versus the faith

It is also helpful to see that the Bible differentiates between 'faith' which reaches out to God and receives from him and 'the faith'. Members of the early church, referring to Paul, said, 'He who formerly persecuted us now preaches *the faith* which he once tried to destroy' (Galatians 1:23). We also read that 'The word of God spread, and the number of the disciples multiplied greatly in Jerusalem, and a great many of the priests were obedient to *the faith*' (Acts 6:7). We are then told in verse 8 that Stephen was 'full of faith'. The church adhered to 'the faith' but Stephen, 'full of faith and power, did great wonders and signs among the people'.

As the church rapidly grew, the early Christians codified their beliefs and put down the foundational, fundamental teaching. We would probably call it church doctrines; they called it 'the faith'. Paul exhorted the Philippian church to 'let your conduct be worthy of the gospel of Christ; so that whether I come and see you or am absent, I may hear of your affairs, that you stand fast in one spirit, with one mind striving together for *the faith* of the gospel' (Philippians 1:27). Paul went to Lystra, Iconium and Antioch strengthening the disciples and exhorting them to continue in 'the faith' (Acts 14:22). Jude wrote, 'Beloved, while I was very diligent to write to you concerning our common salvation, I found it necessary to write to you exhorting you to contend earnestly for *the faith* which was once for all delivered to the saints. For certain men have crept in unnoticed, who long ago were marked out for this condemnation, ungodly men, who turn the grace of our God into licentiousness and deny the only Lord God and our Lord Jesus Christ' (Jude:3–4).

'The faith' is our foundation. If we have not got firm foundations, we will easily be shaken.

Licence versus legalism versus life

The New Testament refers to two extremes: 'licence' and 'legalism'. Licence does unscriptural or un-Christlike things, excusing the actions with the words, 'God told me to do this.' *Rhema* is always subject to *logos*. God will only communicate to us that which is in line with the totality of his word. This is our safeguard as we listen to God. Jude wrote of some who had rejected 'the faith', and had fallen into heresy. To seek guidance over things about which God has already told us in his word is to open ourselves to deception.

The other extreme is legalism. For many Christianity is little more than theory, a set of codified beliefs. Without a constant flow of faith, even with sound doctrines, our Christianity will be dead and lifeless.

How we need constant encounters with the Lord in his word, for we cannot have a clear faith that receives from God without a clear word from him. As we have seen, we cannot be in faith in areas where we do not know God's will, for 'faith comes by hearing and hearing by the word of God' (Romans 10:17). God's word settles any issues.

Firstly, I hear God's promise.

Secondly, I believe him.

Thirdly, I see the results.

4

Living in Sin

The term 'living in sin' has come to be associated with a certain type of moral sin. However, the Bible tells us that 'whatever is not from faith is sin' (Romans 14:23).

It is possible to be living a morally sound lifestyle, yet still be 'living in sin' because of unbelief in our hearts. Unbelief is a serious thing for it calls God a liar. It says, 'I know that you said you would do certain things, but I do not believe that you will.' There is only one remedy for any sin, including unbelief, and that is repentance. We must come and say, 'Lord, forgive me for my unbelief. Change my attitude.' Then we must go to his word and seek for faith to come.

An atmosphere of unbelief

I believe that there is an atmosphere of unbelief in our land which is hindering our seeing many outstanding miracles. God holds the church responsible for this. He does not hold the unsaved responsible for this atmosphere of unbelief. He does not expect them to believe his word, but he does expect us to! Judgement must begin in the house of God.

When Jesus entered Nazareth, 'He could do no mighty work there, except that he laid his hands on a few sick people and healed them. And he marvelled because of their unbelief' (Mark 6:5–6). Over recent years, we have seen a few sick folk healed in this country. But, how we need that 'mighty work'! The only way forward is for us to repent of any unbelief in our lives and let God deal with any hardness of heart, going to his word, that faith might 'come' and replace our unbelief.

I have often noticed two very different kinds of reaction in people as they listen to a testimony. Some get excited and even though they may be aware of a little doubt in their own heart, they want to believe and want to see the same kind of miracles. They say, 'Lord, I want faith to believe like that.' There are others, though, who refuse to believe. They say such things as, 'I bet their healing won't last.' I would define the difference as a longing unbelief and a sceptical unbelief.

A longing unbelief

A longing unbelief was manifest in the father of the demon-possessed boy, who on hearing Jesus' words, 'If you can believe, all things are possible to him who believes,' immediately 'cried out and said with tears "Lord, I believe; help my unbelief!"'(Mark 9:23–24).

This man came to Jesus 'crying'. He was aware that his unbelief was sin. When I hear such cruel accusations as, 'If you had faith, your relative would not have died', I ask the question, 'Where was the accuser's faith in the situation?'

Although Jesus rebuked Thomas for his unbelief, he

did not condemn him but encouraged his faith. Thomas was into the 'seeing is believing' philosophy: 'Unless I see him, I won't believe!' Jesus invited him to examine his wounds (John 20:27–29). Maybe you have some little nagging doubts. Recognize that it is sin and ask the Lord to forgive you; then go to his word that he might give you faith to deal with that longing unbelief. God does not require great faith of us. Mountains can be moved by mustard seed faith (Matthew 17:20). I am told that the mustard seed is the smallest seed in the world.

There have been times when I have said, 'Lord, I find it hard to imagine any change in this situation and that you could do something, but I want to believe you. I choose to believe your word.'

Sceptical unbelief

There are, of course, those who refuse to believe. Jesus said to the religious leaders of his day, that, even if the dead were raised, they would not believe! (see Luke 16:31). They had chosen not to believe and had hardened their hearts. The Bible always holds us responsible for a hard heart. Perhaps you need to search your own heart to see whether you have got 'hardening of the arteries' in any area.

An obvious example is that many Christians have refused to believe what God has been doing through the charismatic movement. Although some have genuinely been frightened by extremes, the fact is that many of the churches where the leaders are moving in things of the Spirit are doubling and trebling in membership, while many of the churches who have resisted these things are having to close down or are keeping their doors open for a few elderly folk. Those same leaders who have rejected and even banned any use of the gifts of the Spirit, or exuberance in praise or worship, then complain when all the lively Christians leave and join another church. Rather than seeking God to discover why the people have needed to move, they simply excuse the mass exodus by accusing the new leaders of 'sheep stealing'.

Those with sceptical unbelief ignore the fact that ministers who have been baptized in the Spirit, even though they may be preaching the same messages as before, are now seeing people getting saved and meeting with God. Despite numerous miraculous healings, people still refuse to believe. Gamaliel, a prominent Jewish leader, gave some very good advice when he said of the early Christians, 'keep away from these men and let them alone; for if this plan or this work is of men, it will come to nothing; but if it is of God, you cannot overthrow it' (Acts 5:38–39).

As a fairly new Christian, I remember being told, 'God does not heal the sick today', to which I replied, 'It's too late; I've already been healed!'

When Jesus attended the synagogue in Nazareth, some were astonished and said, 'Where did this man get this wisdom and these mighty works? Is this not the carpenter's son? Is not his mother called Mary? And his brothers James, Joses, Simon, and Judas? And his sisters, are they not with us? Where then did this man get all these things? So they were offended at him' (Matthew 13:54–57). They chose not to believe. They had a scornful unbelief. We could rationalize everything away if we wanted to. But I have chosen to believe God and have proved his faithfulness. Although these reactions from Jesus' contemporaries were ridiculous, similar ones are sadly still rampant today among so-called 'Evangelical Fundamentalists'.

It is amazing how people will even try and destroy evidence, rather than simply believe. After Lazarus had been raised from the dead, 'Many of the Jews who had come to Mary, and had seen the things Jesus did, believed in him. But some of them went away to the Pharisees and told them the things Jesus had done. Then the chief priests and the Pharisees gathered a council and said, "What shall we do? For this man works many signs. If we let him alone like this, everyone will believe in him, and the Romans will come and take away both our place and nation"... then from that day on, they plotted to put him to death' (John 11:45–46, 53).

We read of rebellious Israel, speaking against the Lord saying,

> 'Can God prepare a table in the wilderness?
> Behold, he struck the rock,
> So that the waters gushed out,
> And the streams overflowed.
> Can he give bread also?
> Can he provide meat for his people?'
> Therefore the Lord heard this and was furious;
> So a fire was kindled against Jacob,
> And anger also came up against Israel,
> Because they did not believe in God,
> And did not trust in his salvation.
>
> Psalm 78:19–22

We are held responsible for any unbelief in our lives. Since we are responsible for a hard heart we need to repent of it and to ask God to soften our hearts and give us faith.

'It is the way I am'

Some people try to excuse unbelief. They say things like, 'It is the way I am! I'm a pessimist by nature.' Well then, get saved! The Bible tells us that when we are born again, we become 'new creatures'. The 'new creature' is not a pessimist!

They may say 'But it runs in the family.' This may be true, but you are now part of a new family. 'Old things have passed away; behold *all* things have become new!' (2 Corinthians 5:17). *Stop confessing what you were and start confessing what you are now in Christ.* So often we destroy our faith by the words we speak.

The power of unbelief

I recently received this letter which demonstrates both God's power to heal and the power of unbelief:

> 'Two years ago, I was playing squash and badly injured my right wrist. I had it X-rayed approximately three months after the event and was informed by the bone specialists at the Queen Elizabeth Hospital, Gateshead, that two fractures were evident and that arthritis was the cause of the continuous pain I was feeling in my wrist. They said that nothing could be done to cure this, apart from taking pain-killing tablets. The pain was aggravated by the daily use of my wrist when driving, writing and occasionally playing squash, when I was forced to bandage the affected wrist tightly for support.
>
> I visited a meeting at a local church in Felling where Peter preached his message to the congregation and then asked for people to whom the Lord had spoken to step forward and commit their lives to the Lord. I was the first to respond, eager to meet the Lord. Peter also

prayed with me for my ailment and the Lord touched me that night, sending a warm glow over my wrist which lasted approximately twenty-four hours. On my departure from the meeting, the devil stepped in and the words I received were that even if my wrist was not cured I would still believe in the Lord and his gift to me of saving my soul. My wrist instantly stiffened and fear prevented me from using it for three days. The devil knew that if the wrist appeared to be defective, then my faith would be in shreds.

Sure enough, the devil had stepped in and the wrist appeared to be worse than ever. I was in the depths of despair and believed the Lord had let me down. Four to five months later, I re-visited the doctor and sought his medical advice. He suggested a further X-ray which I quickly attended and I agreed to a minor operation to fuse the joints of the fractures. By this time, my wrist was worse than ever and I visited the doctor several weeks later to find the results of the new X-rays. The results proved positively that the fractures had been miraculously fused and no presence of any type of fracture were evident in the X-ray. Once the doctor's words were spoken, my wrist ceased to ache, God has proved to me in black and white that He cured me. I warn all Christians to beware of the devil, for he will try his best to rob you of what is rightfully yours!

B.T.
Gateshead, Tyne and Wear[1]

For too long, unbelief has hindered our seeing the miracles of God. Dispensationalism, which teaches that miracles have ceased, is a cover up for unbelief and spiritual impotency. If certain parts of the Bible are 'not for today', who decides which bits are to be excluded? If God has changed his mind concerning

[1] Used with permission

miracles and healing, how do we know that he has not changed his mind about heaven?

God has not changed his mind and his word stands firm. Take the miraculous out of Christianity and we are left with a shaven Samson—powerless.

As I write this chapter, I am in the midst of a crusade in Dar Es Salaam, Tanzania, where hundreds are turning to Christ. Over two thousand have responded in seven days! A little lame girl, unable to walk from birth and brought by her mother, walked perfectly and unaided in the name of Jesus. A boy, dumb from birth, spoke for the first time. His paralysed left arm was also completely healed and he was able to squeeze my hand. Earlier today his Muslim grandmother came to see me, saying, 'I want to know the Jesus that healed my grandchild.' We led her to Christ and she discarded her black Muslim gown and purchased a beautiful white one with flowers on. She also threw away the potions which the witch doctor had given her.

A man with a chronic stutter was healed and spoke clearly. During the seven days, seventeen deaf and fifteen blind people have been instantly healed and at least two men saw for the first time in their lives! These are not just Bible stories, they are still happening today! When I told the people in Africa that God heals the sick today, they believed me and were healed.

5

Unbelievable

When Jesus departed from there, two blind men followed him, crying out and saying, 'Son of David, have mercy on us!' And when he had come into the house, the blind men came to him. And Jesus said to them, '*Do you believe that I am able to do this?*' They said to him, 'Yes, Lord.' Then he touched their eyes, saying, 'According to your faith let it be to you.' And their eyes were opened. And Jesus sternly warned them, saying, 'See that no one knows it.' But when they had departed, they spread the news about him in all that country.

Matthew 9:27

The story is told of a woman who was admiring the Alps from her window whilst on holiday in Switzerland. Remembering Jesus' words, 'If you say to this mountain, "Be removed and be cast into the sea," it will be done', she shouted, 'Be removed and cast into the sea!' Then she shut her blinds and went to bed. The next morning she opened the blinds, to be greeted by the mountain, still there, to which she commented, 'That's just what I expected.'

The blind men who came to Jesus got what they believed for too! Faith and our imagination are connected. If you cannot imagine God doing something, you do not have faith for it. Do you expect your prayers to be answered?

Jesus said, 'Whatever you ask in prayer, *believing*, you will receive' (Matthew 21:22). When Jesus asked people, 'Do you believe that I can do this? He was saying, 'Do you expect me to do this? Can you visualize me doing this?'

You have got to start somewhere

Don't be crushed by men of faith who share tremendous testimonies of mighty miracles. Use your faith to reach out for smaller things and then as you discover God's faithfulness in those smaller things, your faith will grow to reach out for greater things. I did not begin by praying for the blind and the lame to be healed. I started praying for friends who had headaches, back pains, and colds! There is an old Chinese proverb that says, 'A journey of a thousand miles begins with one step.' As I proved God's faithfulness in those small things, my faith grew and my imagination was broadened.

Also my faith grew as I watched other Christians praying for miracles. I sometimes still try to attend meetings taken by other ministers and evangelists who are mightily used by God, for I want to learn and let my faith grow stronger. Once I have seen the Lord perform a certain miracle, I find it a lot easier to pray in faith the next time I am faced with a similar situation. I seek to be in places where the word of God is proclaimed in power and where faith is going to 'come'.

Reading the biblical accounts of God's miracle working power can increase our faith capacity too. If

Jesus did it two thousand years ago, he can do it today! He is 'the same yesterday, today and for ever' (Hebrews 13:8).

Memory lane

I used to keep a note book with the things that I prayed for written on one side of the page, and the other side left blank to write down when and how God answered them. This helped me to 'count my blessings', one by one. Sometimes when we are feeling a bit down, we need to take a trip down Memory Lane and remind ourselves of God's faithfulness in the past.

I found it hard to believe that he would heal me

I used to have a lot of unsightly warts on my right arm. I had tried all kinds of ways to get rid of them. Before I was saved, I had gone to a wart charmer, not realizing that such things are condemned in God's word (see Deuteronomy 18:9–14). I had also been to the doctor's and had them burnt off, but they soon grew again. After my conversion to Christ I knew, through reading the Scriptures, that God could heal. I also believed that God wanted to heal all who were sick. But I still found it hard to believe that he would heal me!

I could not imagine God healing me of such a minor thing, when there were so many people who had much greater needs than I. My conscience also told me that it was only vanity that wanted to get rid of them. So I decided I would have to live with them. However, during a crusade service I attended, as various people testified to what God had done in their lives, a little girl came forward to the microphone and said, 'I had a wart on my knee and Jesus has healed me.' When she said that, my faith erupted! My expectation grew! For the first time, I could imagine God healing me. So I went forward and was prayed for. Although the warts were still there, I knew my healing was on the way. That night, as I was travelling home, I suddenly remembered that years before I had been to the wart charmer and so I said to the brother driving me home, 'Do you believe that going to a wart charmer, even before I was saved, could prevent me receiving the healing?'

He replied, 'Yes, I do.' At that, I asked the Lord to forgive me for going to the charmer and my friend prayed for me, cutting off the effect of that past occult contact.

The next morning, when I woke up, every single wart had gone!

Hoping and praying

So many Christians say, 'I'll pray and see if anything happens.' Another common term is, 'I'm hoping and praying that something will happen.' Usually such prayers will be disappointed, for although faith and hope are complementary, they are very different. Faith is for the now, whereas hope is 'future faith'. Faith reaches into the unseen and brings it into our experience; hope confidently looks to the future. It is to do with things to come (see Romans 8:22–25). Hope assures us of Christ's return, encourages us to keep going despite the trials and tribulations of life and provokes us to godliness: 'For the grace of God that brings salvation has appeared to all men, teaching us that, denying ungodliness and worldly lusts, we should live soberly, righteously, and godly in the present age, *looking for the blessed hope* and glorious appearing of our great God and Saviour Jesus Christ' (Titus 2:11–13).

Our blessed hope is Christ's coming and our eternal home is glory. Biblical hope has nothing to do with the modern word hope—which is wishful thinking and means that something might happen but there is a chance that it will not: 'I hope you have a lovely holiday.' 'I hope you get nice weather.' 'I hope you get healed.' 'I hope everything works out well.' These common statements really mean, 'There is a good chance it will not!' The New Testament hope is a certainty which brings security.

Many Christians confuse faith with this worldly type of hope and usually go away disappointed! Even biblical hope is different from faith, for I cannot use my faith to bring Christ back today, but I know that he will return. Faith brings the unseen into the realm of the seen. Praying without faith is ineffective.

Believing is seeing

The miracles Jesus performed were not just a sovereign God intervening and doing whatever he liked. People reached out to the Lord in faith. It was to faith that he responded.

Jesus said to the leper, '"Go your way; your faith has made you well." And immediately he received his sight' (Mark 10:52).

To the centurion Jesus said '"Go your way; and as *you have believed*, so let it be done for you." And his servant was healed that same hour' (Matthew 8:13).

Jesus touched the eyes of the two blind men saying, '"According to *your faith* let it be to you." And their eyes were opened' (Matthew 9:29).

To the woman with the issue of blood, Jesus said, '"Be of good cheer, daughter; *your faith has made you well.*" And the woman was made well from that hour' (Matthew 9:22).

We have already seen that it is faith that makes prayer work, not eloquence. *Unbelief binds God's hand.* When the disciples asked Jesus why they were unable to cast the demon out of the boy, Jesus replied, '*Because of your unbelief*; for assuredly, I say to you, if you have faith as a mustard seed, you will say to this mountain, "Move from here to there," and it will move; and nothing will be impossible for you' (Matthew 17:20). It was because of unbelief that Israel was not permitted to enter the promised land. In Nazareth Jesus could do no mighty work 'because of their unbelief' (Matthew 13:58). God was not unwilling to perform mighty miracles in Nazareth. In the case of the demon-possessed boy Jesus proved that it was God's will for him to be healed. When a miracle we have prayed for does not take place, we cannot point the finger at God and say, 'It was obviously not his will.' We can blame the preacher or we can blame other people, but God says, 'Be it unto you according to *your faith.*' *God's only limitations are the ones that we put on him.*

Wrong believing

Unbelief is not a lack of believing. It is wrong believing. Unbelief has been described as 'faith in reverse gear'. God has given to every man a measure of faith. You can put your faith in the word of God and go forward or you can put your faith in the information your circumstances give you, what the devil whispers in your ear, or other people's experiences or opinions. *Unbelief expects negative things*. When all the calamities came upon Job, he said, 'for the thing I greatly feared has come upon me' (Job 3:25). He got what he believed for! In the same way that faith attracts positive things into our lives, unbelief attracts negative things. Unbelief is as destructive as faith is constructive.

The right side of the law

I used to have a fear of the police. I would be driving along quite happily in my car but the moment I saw a police car I would begin to worry. I would worry in case my brake lights had failed or I had exceeded the speed limit. Whenever I saw the police, I was convinced that they were going to stop me. Since I believed it, I used to be continually stopped. I am convinced that if I had gone to court just as a witness or as part of the jury, I would have pleaded guilty!

Once I was stopped because they thought I was stealing a car! On another occasion I was arrested for breaking and entering during a crusade! A friend locked the church hall keys in his car, so we tried to get in by using a knife on the Yale lock. Nine policemen were sent to arrest us and three police cars parked around the van, in case we tried to escape! The sergeant said over his walkie-talkie as we were thrown up against the van, 'We've caught the intruders and we are bringing them in!' The escorted journey to the station with the lights flashing was quite traumatic and it took a lot to convince the police that we were supposed to be at the church! Already that day the police had threatened to arrest me for causing an obstruction when a large crowd gathered during an open-air meeting.

However, eventually I began to see that I was believing for these negative things to happen. When I repented of my fears and asked someone to pray with me that God would set me free, he did.

Why not?

The first time I took my driving text, I went in fear. I was convinced that I was going to fail. When I left the test centre and the examiner said, 'Turn left, Mr Gammons', I turned right! I was not at all surprised when he failed me. However, before I took it again, someone came up to me and said, 'I believe that God has shown me that you are going to pass.' I was prepared to accept that they could be wrong, but my faith began to rise.

I thought, 'Why not?' and began to pray, 'Lord, I have a couple of lessons left before my next test. If there are any mistakes I am still making that need dealing with, show my driving instructor so that he can correct them.' Then I went to that driving test expecting to pass. My mental attitude was so changed that I went relaxed, actually enjoyed the test and passed!

What could you believe God for? What could you imagine God doing? Once at a conference, Don Double, the leader of Good News Crusade, shared how God had told someone to give him a new car. As I listened, my faith began to rise, my expectations grew and my imagination was broadened. At the end of the meeting, I walked up to Don and said, 'I am going to drive my new car home by faith.'

At that time I had no idea how God would provide or when, but inside I knew that he would. So, although I drove my old car home, by faith I was driving my new one! The next time I saw Don, about two months later, I turned up in my new car, which God had told someone to give me!

I later shared this at a meeting I was speaking at and one of the ministers there, who had a very old car, found his faith beginning to rise and said, 'Lord, if you can do that for him, I believe that you can do it for me.' A couple of weeks later, he unexpectedly came into some money and so he was able to buy a new car.

Use your faith. Of course, it is no use to pray for a new car if you could not even imagine God providing you with an old one. Most new car owners began with an old one! What can you believe God for now? We have to begin somewhere. The answer may not always be instantaneous. On most occasions I have believed for things one pound at a time!

What can *you* imagine God doing?

6

Presenting Your Case

Did you realize that God can be moved by a good argument?

He has made us in his image, as rational beings. When challenging Israel, who had no excuse for their sin, God still invited them, saying, '"Present your case," says the Lord. "Bring forth your strong reasons," says the King of Jacob' (Isaiah 41:21).

That does not mean that we can twist God's arm, nor am I talking about disagreeing with God and his word, but I am saying that the Lord likes to know that we believe what we are asking for. We can even find people in Scripture who came to God with a good argument and convinced Him!

> Abraham came and said, 'Lord, you're going to judge these people. If you can find fifty righteous people, will you not judge them?'
>
> So the Lord says, 'Okay, Abraham, for fifty righteous people.'
>
> Next Abraham said, 'What's five people, Lord? For forty-five people you wouldn't judge them, would you?'
>
> So the Lord says 'Okay, if I can find forty-five righteous people, I won't judge them.'

So Abraham says, 'What is ten between friends? How about thirty people, Lord? If there are thirty righteous people, you wouldn't judge them, would you? You are a merciful God.'

So the Lord agreed, 'Okay, for thirty righteous I will not destroy them.'

'Twenty?' Abraham proposed.

'Yes, okay,' the Lord replied. 'Twenty people.'

Next, Abraham says, 'Well, Lord, if you are going down as low as twenty, you might as well go down to ten.'

I think Abraham would have made a great car salesman!

God says, 'Okay then, you have made your point. If there are ten righteous people, I won't judge them.'

Genesis 18:16–33, Gammons' paraphrase version

Abraham was not presumptuous. He was not trying to get God to do something against his will. He knew God's heart, that he did not want to judge people and so Abraham stood in the gap.

When Samson, a man once mightily anointed by God, was about to die as a result of his sin, he prayed, 'Strengthen me, I pray, just this once' (Judges 16:28). Just give me one more chance. And the Lord did.

Once, because Israel had sinned and worshipped a golden calf, God was prompted to destroy them, but for forty days and forty nights Moses prevailed in prayer (Deuteronomy 9:18). He said things like, 'Lord, blot my name out of your book if you are going to judge them. Don't destroy your people and your inheritance whom you have redeemed in your greatness, whom you brought out of Egypt with a mighty hand. Lord, you brought them out of Egypt. Now don't destroy them or you will have wasted your time. Remember your covenant with Abraham, Isaac and Jacob.'

The Lord said to Moses, 'Let me alone, that I may destroy them' (Deuteronomy 9:14). Yet when Moses said 'No, Lord, don't destroy them,' the Lord did not destroy them and the destiny of a nation was saved by a good argument from a man who was persistent because he knew what he wanted and he was not going to give up.

'Ask, and it will be given to you; seek, and you will find; knock, and it will be opened to you' (Luke 11:9). The Greek text uses the present continuous tense: 'Ask and keep on asking, and it shall be given to you. Seek and keep on seeking, and you shall find. Knock and keep on knocking, and the door will be opened to you.'

Jesus told a story about a widow who persistently sought vindication from a judge (Luke 18:1–8). She did not give in, she fully expected to win, for faith does not give up. The judge was moved by her constant expectation. There is a place for persistence in prayer. God is moved by our persistent expectation, as long as it is in faith. If we are not praying in faith, we can continue praying for something for years and never see the results. But believing is seeing.

Jesus gave another example. A man who had unexpected guests and no food for them, knocked on his sleeping neighbour's door. His neighbour, unimpressed by his timing, said, 'Go away; I'm in bed.' However, the man eventually received bread from his neighbour, because of his importunity, because he held on (Luke 11:5–8).

Victory!

Daniel, an Old Testament man of God and a respected politician, was praying for his people to be delivered from captivity. Gabriel, the angel, was sent to encourage him (Daniel 9:21–23). Gabriel explained that right from the moment Daniel had started praying his prayer had been heard and that the delay was not because God was unwilling, but because there was opposition in the heavenlies from the powers of darkness.

Sometimes in prayer we are called to battle to take territory. The victory has already been settled, Satan is a defeated foe, so don't give up. Jesus is victor!

I received a letter the other day, concerning a spiritist who on a number of occasions had advertised meetings near where my correspondent lived. The churches in that city prayed together against the visits and every time she has tried to come, for some reason her trip had to be cancelled! The woman also said in her letter that all the churches had got together and prayed against a cult which had its headquarters in the city and now they have closed down too. We can see mighty victories in prayer, if we do not give up.

7

Faith at the Crossroads

Now when Jesus had crossed over again by boat to the other side, a great multitude gathered to him; and he was by the sea. And behold, one of the rulers of the synagogue came, Jairus by name. And when he saw him, he fell at his feet and begged him earnestly saying, 'My little daughter lies at the point of death. Come and lay your hands on her, that she may be healed, and she will live.' So Jesus went with him, and a great multitude followed him and thronged him.

Now a certain woman had a flow of blood for twelve years, and had suffered many things from many physicians. She had spent all that she had and was no better, but rather grew worse. When she heard about Jesus, she came behind him in the crowd and touched his garment; for she said, 'If only I may touch his clothes, I shall be made well.' Immediately the fountain of her blood was dried up, and she felt in her body that she was healed of the affliction.

And Jesus, immediately knowing in himself that power had gone out of him, turned around in the crowd and said, 'Who touched my clothes?' But his disciples said to him, 'You see the multitude thronging you, and you say "Who touched me?"' And he looked around to see her who had done this thing. But the woman, fearing and trembling, knowing what had happened to her, came and fell down before him and told him the whole truth. And he said to her, 'Daughter, your faith has made you well. Go in peace, and be healed of your affliction.'

While he was still speaking, some came from the ruler of the synagogue's house who said, 'Your daughter is dead. Why trouble the Teacher any further?' As soon as Jesus heard the word that was spoken, he said to the ruler of the synagogue, 'Do not be afraid; only believe.' And he permitted no one to follow him except Peter, James and John the brother of James.

Then he came to the house of the ruler of the synagogue, and saw a tumult and those who wept and wailed loudly. When he came in, he said to them, 'Why make this commotion and weep? The child is not dead, but sleeping.' And they laughed him to scorn. But when he had put them all out, he took the father and the mother of the child, and those who were with him, and entered where the child was lying. Then he took the child by the hand, and said to her, 'Talitha, cumi,' which is translated, 'Little girl, I say to you, arise.' Immediately the girl arose and walked, for she was twelve years of age. And they were overcome with great amazement. But he commanded them strictly that no one should know it, and said that something should be given her to eat.

Mark 5:21–43

Each one of us has faith, because 'God has dealt to each one a measure of faith' (Romans 12:3). But, as we have seen, the issue is not whether we have enough faith, but what we do with our faith; where we put it. Jairus came to Jesus, probably having heard of the miracles that he had been performing, and begged him saying, 'My little daughter lies at the point of death. Come and lay your hands on her, that she may be healed, and she will live.' That was a confession of faith. There was no doubt in his mind that if Jesus would come his child would be healed! It is only faith that opens the door for God to work in a situation.

As I write this, I am reminded of a visit to Africa. I had been speaking at a meeting of the political leaders of the country and other dignitaries. At the end of the meeting, one of the leading dignitaries, who was not a Christian, came up to me and said, 'Will you pray for my child? He is at the point of death in hospital with malaria.' Very few children who get malaria live, especially young children, because they have not built up any natural immunity or resistance to the disease. So there and then we prayed together that the Lord would touch and heal that child and I rebuked the malaria in the name of Jesus. Immediately afterwards the man left for the hospital.

The next evening at the end of the meeting, he came up to me and said, 'I wanted to come and thank you. When I got to the hospital my child was sitting up in bed. He had eaten a meal and was playing with his toys! He was completely healed, and they even released him from hospital last night! The nurses told me the time at which he had amazingly recovered: it was the same time we had prayed together. I want to know more about this Jesus who has healed my child.'

Jesus has not changed! He has the same power today to do the same things that he did two thousand years ago! He is the same 'today' as he was 'yesterday' and he will be 'for ever' (Hebrews 13:8).

Crossroads no. 1

Can you visualize the urgency of the situation as Jairus pushes through the crowd to get to Jesus? 'I've got to get to him quickly, because my child is dying.' As he reaches Jesus, he falls down before him, begging Jesus to come quickly. Together they set off towards the man's house. But as they travel, the man's faith comes to a crossroads, to a situation where the information his outward circumstances are giving him points in a different direction from the information that Jesus' words are giving to him.

OUTWARD CIRCUMSTANCES	JESUS' WORDS
'Your daughter is dead. Why trouble the Teacher any further?' (verse 35)	'Do not be afraid; only believe.' (verse 36)

What was he going to put his faith in, Jesus' words or his outward circumstances? He knew that Jesus could heal the sick, but could he raise the dead? The messenger was saying, 'I wouldn't bother Jesus. This situation is too big for him. It is out of his reach. If you had got here in time, the child could have been healed, but now it's gone too far for even Jesus to do anything.'

His outward circumstances said, 'It must have been God's will that she died. You will just have to accept the situation.' But faith takes God at his word and says, 'God said it, that settles it!' We too are frequently faced with this challenge, where we can use our faith to believe God or to believe the information that our outward circumstances are giving us. Nothing is too hard for the Lord! Sometimes we judge a situation by what we think would be easy or hard for him. Yet as we have said, a headache is no easier for the Lord to heal than a cancer! He is almighty!

The messenger said, 'Why trouble the Teacher any further?' What we need to realize is that it was no trouble, for Jesus had voluntarily agreed to come, because he cared for the man and he cared for the child. God cares about you, too!

It was the same for the woman with the issue of blood. When she saw the size of the crowd she could have said, 'It's obviously not God's will for me to be healed. I've tried all the medication that I can get and that has done me no good and now there's such a crowd. I'm probably wasting my time.' However, the Bible says that she moved through the crowd, saying, 'If only I may touch his clothes, I shall be made well.' Her outward circumstances said, 'Give in.' But faith does not give in. She knew that Jesus was on the side of health!

God desires us to prosper and be in health even as our soul prospers (3 John 2). God wants you as physically well as he wants you spiritually well—a hundred per cent.

Jesus came to show us what God is like. He said, 'He who has seen me has seen the Father' (John 14:9). *If you ever doubt God's will concerning health, look at Jesus.* Did he turn anyone away who came in faith? Only one person, a leper who came to Jesus, questioned God's will concerning healing, 'If you will, you can make me clean.' Jesus instantly replied, 'I am willing; be cleansed' (Mark 1:40–41). If an angel appeared to me and said, 'Jesus does not heal the sick today,' I would call him a liar and a heretic because the Bible says that even angels are subject to the word of God. God has said it; that settles it! His word will never pass away. It is eternally established.

Crossroads no. 2

Jairus had been faced with the first crossroads and continued to believe Jesus' words. Now he encountered the next crossroads.

OUTWARD CIRCUMSTANCES	JESUS' WORDS
Then he came to the house of the ruler of the synagogue, and saw a tumult and those who wept and wailed loudly. (verse 38)	'The child is not dead, but sleeping.' (Verse 39)

When Jairus arrived at his home, he heard the official mourners, who were paid to weep and wail. His outward circumstances said, 'You're wasting your time. The child is dead.' Jesus' words declared, 'The child is not dead, but sleeping.' As one translation puts it, 'The child is not beyond the reach of faith.'

Sometimes we are more inclined to believe our outward circumstances and to accept our problems than we are to believe God's word. But if God said it, that settles it!

God's logic

Our mind will question whatever God promises and seek to elevate itself over the word of God. God's assessment of our common sense is 'The whole head is sick' (Isaiah 1:5).

So often God's promises seem like a paradox. For example, common sense says, 'Give and you will have less.' God says, 'Give, and it will be given to you: good measure, pressed down, shaken together, and running over' (Luke 6:38). You cannot out-give God.

Common sense says, 'Try a bit harder.' But God's word says, 'Come to me...and you will find rest' (Matthew 6:28–29). 'Casting all your care upon him, for he cares for you' (1 Peter 5:7). He did not make you to be a weight-lifter!

The word of God says, 'Praise him in everything.' Common sense says, 'Wait until you see a change. Wait until you feel differently.'

'The foolishness of God is wiser than men' (1 Corinthians 1:25). The outward circumstances of Abraham and Sarah said, 'You are wasting your time. It is impossible to have a child now.' But God's word said, 'You are going to have a child' (Genesis 17:17–22). When their faith came to the crossroads, they followed God's word.

Imagine the information Peter's outward circumstances gave him when Jesus invited him to walk on the waters. The spray hit him in the face, and waves were being blown about by the wind, but he chose to believe Jesus' word (Matthew 14:29–30).

OUTWARD CIRCUMSTANCES	JESUS' WORDS
'I do not feel or look healed.'	By whose stripes you were healed. (1 Peter 2:24)

Our outward circumstances may say after prayer, 'You do not look healed. You do not feel healed.' Jesus' word says, 'By Christ's stripes, you *were* healed.' Not, 'There is a possibility you *might* be healed', but, you *were* healed. By faith I received my inheritance, that which is already mine. God revealed himself to Israel saying, 'I am the Lord that healeth thee' (Exodus 15:26). 'Thee' means *me*.

On one occasion I was at a meeting where a man was carried in. Although he had crutches, he had no strength in his legs. In his late seventies, he was also deaf and diabetic. At the end of the meeting, I prayed with him and God healed the diabetes, as the hospital later confirmed. He was also instantly healed of his deafness, for he could hear people talking from the other end of the room and repeat what they were saying. However, friends helped him out of the meeting in the same way that they had helped him in. He looked no different, and I'm convinced that there were people in the meeting who were disappointed. Nevertheless, he went by faith. Feelings follow facts and his body had to catch up with his faith. By the end of the week, he had thrown away his crutches, bought himself a bike and could be seen cycling around the town!

OUTWARD CIRCUMSTANCES	JESUS' WORDS
'I have no money.'	'My God shall supply all your needs according to his riches in glory.' (Philippians 4:19)

Our outward circumstances may say, 'You have not got any money.' But God's word says, 'My God shall supply *all* your needs.' Who is your God? He is the Alpha and the Omega, the almighty One, the One to whom everything is 'him-possible'. He *shall* (not might) supply, *all* (not some) of your needs.

I love the way the account of Jairus' daughter closes with Jesus saying, 'Give her some food.' How practical! For many people, this would seem totally unspiritual. Probably the last thing most Christians would think about, after seeing a dead child raised, is food! But Jesus cares about your practical needs!

8

Feelings Follow Facts

Sometimes the information which our bodies and our feelings give us has to catch up with the word of God. My faith has to give me the information.

Three cats were walking along a wall. The one in front was named 'Fact', the one in the middle 'Faith', and the last one was called 'Feelings'. While 'Faith' kept his eyes on 'Fact' he walked happily along the wall. When he turned around to see how 'Feelings' was, he fell off!

What have you got your eyes on, the facts or your feelings?

If God said it, it must be true, for his word is true (John 17:17). *By faith, we can have something, before we actually experience it and before we actually get our hands on it.*

At one time I needed a caravan for our camp work and so I phoned someone whom I trust in that particular area and said, 'I'd like you to get me a caravan.' He phoned me a couple of days later and said, 'I've got you a caravan, so please send me the money.' I had to trust him, that he really had a caravan for me. When I wrote out the cheque, I was trusting him.

Someone came up to me before I had collected it,

and said, 'I hear you need a caravan.'

But I was able to say, 'I've already got one.'

He said, 'Oh, what's it like?'

I had to reply, 'Well, I don't know, I haven't seen it yet. But it's mine.' The fact was it had been purchased for me. 'It is mine and I'll be collecting it in two months' time.' I actually had a caravan before I physically experienced the benefit of it.

The Scriptures teach that by Christ's 'stripes you *were healed*' (1 Peter 2:24). Not you *can* be healed, not you *might* be healed, nor tomorrow night Jesus *may* heal you; you already are healed! It is yours by right, because Christ purchased it on the cross. So you are to believe that you have received 'when you pray' not when you see any physical evidence of the answer. Anyone can believe he is healed when there is physical evidence!

Many Christians say, 'If I could see a change, I would believe'. But that is not believing, that is seeing. They say, 'If I could just feel better, I would believe.' That is not believing, that is feeling. You do not believe with your eyes, you see with them. You do not believe with your ears, you hear with them. You do not believe with your feelings, you feel with them. You believe with your heart, it is an internal thing.

People often say, 'I will believe that I am healed, when I feel better.' But that is not faith. It is easy to believe when the pain is gone! Faith always has to operate before you see any evidence. Faith is believing despite any physical evidence. I believe I am going to heaven before I get there. I have never seen heaven, or felt it, but I believe it is a reality. Faith will hold on to God's promises, even when there is no immediate evidence. It will not be thrown or disappointed but will peacefully know that the answer is on the way.

When we are tried, faith says 'I believe', presumption says 'I believed'. Faith holds on—presumption will be disappointed.

Cut off at the root

A felled tree lying on the ground may still have green leaves, but they will not be green for long, for it has been cut off at its life source. But the natural eye sees the leaves and wrongly believes that the tree is in health. In the same way, the natural eye may still see the symptoms (e.g. swollen ankles), but the eye of faith sees us in health, because Christ bore our sicknesses. When Jesus cursed the fig tree, there was no immediate evidence of change, but he could continue on his journey for something had happened, the life of the tree had been cut off (Matthew 21:18–20).

'Faith means we are confident of what we hope for, convinced of what we do not see' (Hebrews 11:1; Moffat's translation).

Many Christians are faced with the dilemma of what to confess in the time between when they receive their healing by faith and when they actually experience the manifestation of it. Faith does not, of course, deny the natural evidence, nor pretend that it is not there. We are not talking about 'mind over matter'. Although faith will admit to the negative physical symptoms, it knows that God's word supersedes them, in the same way that one natural law can supersede another. For example, the law of thrust—throwing an object into the air—is overruled by another law, the law of gravity, which brings objects back down. Just as lawyers, doctors, bankers, scientists and mechanics have their own language, which seems foreign to others, so faith's language seems strange to the natural mind.

The whole truth, and nothing but the truth

There is 'big 'T' Truth' and 'little 't' truth'. Big 'T' Truth is what God says, for he cannot lie. Little 't' truth is what my outward circumstances say. The messenger's words to Jairus, 'Your daughter is dead', were absolutely true, but they were little 't' truth. Jesus said of the girl, 'She is not beyond the reach of faith.' That was big 'T' Truth. When God's word and our outward circumstances differ, I want to get my information from God's word.

Many Christians find it helpful to confess 'By Christ's stripes I am healed', saying that they believe God is at work and will complete the work he has begun.

Some would respond: 'But we must face the facts.' True, but the facts are what God has said, not the things our fears tell us. The more we put our fears into words, the more we become gripped by them. Since God cannot lie, we cannot be lying if we say what God says. If God calls the things that do not exist as though they did (Romans 4:17) why can't I do the same?

Whatever you say, do not confess negative things when you are expecting God to change them. Do not let your words destroy your faith. Bambi's mother gave some good advice in the Walt Disney classic when she said, 'If you can't say anything good, don't say anything at all.'

Can I be prayed for again?

People often say, 'I've already received prayer for healing, can I be prayed for again?' Often the first time we pray, we do not have too much confidence that we are going to be healed, and on subsequent occasions as we are prayed for, our faith grows. If you have renewed faith to be prayed for again, there is no reason why you should not be. However, I see no point in being continually prayed for 'to see if it works this time'.

So when do we stop praying? When we know that we have got through and have the assurance that our answer is on the way, when 'You know, that you know, that you know, that you know.' This is the time when we can begin to thank God that we have received the answer to our prayer.

Thanks, Lord!

'Be anxious for nothing, but in everything by prayer and supplication, *with thanksgiving*, let your requests be made known to God' (Philippians 4:6). Praise can be a real expression of faith. Often Christians become so problem-centred that they are constantly anxious about their own ailments. Praise gets our eyes off our problem and on to the Lord. *It gets our eyes off the mountain and onto the mountain-mover!* I have known many people who have been healed when they least expected it, often when they were caught up in praise and worship, forgetting about their problems. Praise gets our eyes on the Lord. Negative speaking and thanksgiving are incompatible.

Hold fast to the confession of your faith 'without wavering, for he who promised is faithful' (Hebrews 10:23).

9

Hold On

> Then he [Jesus] spoke a parable to them to this end, that men ought always to pray and not lose heart, saying: 'There was in a certain city a judge who did not fear God nor regard man. Now there was a widow in that city; and she came to him, saying, "Avenge me of my adversary." And he would not for a while; but afterwards he said within himself, "Though I do not fear God nor regard man, yet because this widow troubles me, I will avenge her, lest by her continual coming she weary me."' Then the Lord said, 'Hear what the unjust judge said. And shall God not avenge his own elect who cry out day and night to him, *though he bears long with them*? I tell you that he will avenge them speedily. Nevertheless, when the Son of Man comes, *will he really find faith on the earth*?
>
> Luke 18:1–8

Sometimes God 'bears with us' and the answer to our prayer is not immediate; but true faith will not give up. Sometimes God tries us to see whether he will still 'find faith'. Sometimes answers to prayer come quickly, but other times they come slowly. We love the instant answers, but when God tries our faith, it is not quite so popular. However, when we pray in faith, the answer begins its journey to us. Unbelief stops it in its tracks and until we have repented and dealt with unbelief, our answer does not continue its course.

Although our prayers are often not answered instantly, Jesus said, 'Whatever you ask for in prayer, believe that you have received it, and it will be yours' (Mark 11:24, NIV). Believing is seeing. 'For we walk by faith, not by sight' (2 Corinthians 5:7).

'By faith he [Moses] forsook Egypt, not fearing the wrath of the king; for he endured, as *seeing him who is invisible*' (Hebrews 11:27).

Faith sees the invisible. The natural mind or common sense, says, 'Your prayer has not been answered', when the evidence is not instant. But, by faith I can say, 'My miracle is on the way.' Although God has promised to answer prayer and has said that whatever we ask, he will do, we cannot dictate to him how or when he will do it. A very important lesson to learn is that *God's delays are not denials*.

The trying of our faith

Because there is a delay, we should not automatically conclude that it is not God's will. For example, Isaac was promised a son, but between the promise and fulfilment of that promise were years of waiting. Moses was promised he would be the deliverer of God's people but between that call and its realization were forty years of pastoring sheep in the wilderness! (Good preparation for pastoring Israel!)

God promised Israel that Jericho's walls would fall, but first they had to march around the city once a day for six days and seven times on the seventh day (Joshua 6:1–20)! Imagine the conversations among Jericho's inhabitants.

'There's a lot of people marching around the city walls. Any idea who they are?'

'Ha, it's those weird Hebrews. It's amazing what they get up to!'

'What are they doing?'

'Oh, they're just marching around the city, singing. Nothing unusual!'

'Hallo! You lot, religious nuts! What are you doing?'

Can you imagine by the sixth day the kind of abuse they were getting? I can picture the devil whispering, 'You're wasting your time. During the last six days nothing has happened. What do you expect to happen on the seventh day? I hope you've got plenty of shoes, because you're going to be wearing out a lot of shoes in the next fifty years! You may as well give up; you're wasting your time.'

But hang on, Israel; the miracle is on its way. On day seven, as they marched and blew the trumpet, the walls came tumbling down! *Don't give up...hold on...God's timing is perfect.*

Naaman, a great military leader, was sent by the prophet Elijah to dip seven times in the Jordan and was told that he would then be healed. Imagine how he felt when he came out of the water after the sixth time as leprous as ever! You see, it wasn't until the time that God had ordained, when Naaman dipped the seventh time, that he came up whole!

Consider the predicament of the lepers who came to Jesus to be healed. When he sent them to the priest to certify their healing they were as leprous as when they came to him. It was 'as they went' that they were healed (Luke 17:14). This implies a gradual healing on the way to the priest. Their healing did not happen the moment they met the Lord. The priests were the only ones who could certify a person as physically whole and able to go back into society. Can you imagine going to the doctors as sick as you were when you came to Jesus? Can you imagine the devil whispering in their ear, 'All the other people talked about going to Jesus, and being instantly healed, but you are as sick as you ever were. You're wasting your time. If I were you, I wouldn't go to the priest. You'll be stoned before you even get to the city! If I were you, I'd go straight back to the leper colony. Even if you die in pain, you might get a day or two longer to live than if they stone you for going into the city.'

But the lepers continued on their journey in faith. They hung on and as they went, they were healed. They could easily have become disheartened and said, 'It's not going to work.' Instead, they held on to Jesus' promise.

Visiting Siloam on a trip to Israel was a real eye opener to me. After a tiring walk along a dusty road, you must descend a steep flight of steps to reach the water. My first thought was, 'This is the last place you would send a blind man!' I'm sure that there were lots of safer places Jesus could have sent the man, but few better tests of whether he really meant business, for, as he got to the waters and obeyed the Lord, he was healed.

When we pray for healing we may find there is a gradual improvement until we realize, very often unexpectedly, that we have been completely healed.

God cannot lie!

Hebrews 6 exhorts 'do not become sluggish, but imitate those who *through faith and patience inherit the promises*' (6:12). God made a promise to Abraham, saying, 'In blessing I will bless you, and in multiplying I will multiply your descendants (Genesis 22:17). But it was only after he had patiently endured that Abraham obtained the promise. Why did he hold on in faith? It was because he knew that 'it is impossible for God to lie' (Hebrews 6:18). Abraham did not see the immediate results of his faith, but he did know that God could not lie. 'After he had patiently endured, he obtained the promise' (Hebrews 6:15). So many Christians plunge into despondency and self-pity when their prayers are not instantly answered, but Abraham held on.

God had said it—therefore that settled it for Abraham. The time between when you pray the prayer of faith and when you see the physical manifestation of your answers, may be a split second or it may be, as for Abraham, twenty-five years! It is during that waiting period that Satan launches his all-out attack, seeking to stop us 'holding fast to the profession of our faith' (Hebrews 10:23). Would you have held on twenty-five years? Sarah, by faith, 'also received strength to conceive and she bore a child when she was past the age, because she judged him faithful' (Hebrews 11:11). God had said it, so for Sarah that settled it!

'The Lord visited Sarah as he had said, and the Lord did for Sarah as he had spoken. For Sarah conceived and bore Abraham a son in his old age, at the set time of which God had spoken to him' (Genesis 21:1–2). God had a set time and Abraham and Sarah held on in faith until that time.

Faith and patience

Notice that it is by 'faith and *patience*' that we inherit the promises (Hebrews 10:36). *Faith takes hold of God's promise and patience keeps hold! Faith and patience together mean that we believe and continue to believe*. One of the commandments Christians find most difficult to keep is 'Rest in the Lord and wait patiently for him' (Psalm 37:7). Someone said the world's most common prayer is, 'Lord, I want patience and I want it now.' There is a patient trust which knows that God has heard us, and brings a child-like rest in God's fatherly love. 'Do not fret—it only causes harm' (Psalm 37:8). Some people have the idea that faith is something which one has to try and work up: 'I believe, Lord; I believe, Lord; I believe, Lord.' That is not faith. Faith knows what God has said and rests in his faithfulness, believing that 'It is going to be so, because God said it!' True faith can rest in God's faithfulness.

Impatience can so easily get us into trouble. Consider Aaron, who made a false God because Moses was delayed up the mountain (Exodus 32:1), or Saul, who was told to wait seven days for the prophet. After the sixth day, he became impatient and made the sacrifice himself—a costly mistake. Out of Sarah and Abraham's impatience, as they tried to help God out, Ishmael was produced! (Genesis 16:1–16).

Who needs patience when the manifestation of the answer is instantaneous? Waiting patiently requires yielding to God's timetable! God will not be a millionth of a second too soon or too late, as long as we do not allow unbelief to hold up the proceedings. But, sometimes his schedule differs from ours. To be patient means to remain constant, stationary, in the same place. Patience does not surrender to the pressure of a situation; instead it holds fast. It does not lose heart when there is a delay.

Hold on; your miracle is on the way

For over forty years, George Müller prayed for two friends to be saved. One day, referring to this issue, someone challenged him: 'Mr Müller, you say that all your prayers are answered. What do you mean?'

He replied, 'I have prayed for many years for the Lord to bring two I dearly love to Himself. They have not yet accepted Christ as their Saviour, but I know they eventually will come to know him. Therefore, I say, "All my prayers are answered."'

That is an example of expectant but restful faith. Not long after that incident both men gave their lives to Christ. Don't give up. Hold on. Your miracle is on the way!

10

Flying Lessons

Is God worth serving for who he is?

That is a question that spans the ages. The book of Job introduces us to a blameless and upright man who feared God and shunned evil (Job 1:1). Yet Job became the target of Satan's accusations. The devil taunted the Lord, claiming that Job would withdraw his love and service from God if he ceased blessing him. Slyly he asked, 'Does Job fear God for nothing? Stretch out your hand and touch all that he has, and he will surely curse you to your face!' (Job 1:9, 11). In other words, 'Job only serves you for what he is getting out of it.' So God gave Satan freedom to take away Job's family, business, friends, health and his finance. Yet, 'In all of this Job did not sin or charge God with wrong' (Job 1:22).

After these experiences, Job had a revelation of God's power, wisdom and purpose, so that he could say, 'I have heard of you by the hearing of the ear, but now my eye sees you. Therefore I abhor myself, and repent in dust and ashes' (Job 42:5–6). Then, after praying for his 'friends', Job received from God twice as much as he had before. 'Now the Lord blessed the latter days of Job more than his beginning', so that he lived to a ripe age, seeing his children and grandchildren for four generations (Job 42:10, 12, 16, 17). Job came out as living proof that God is worth loving and serving just for who he is!

As Habakkuk the prophet put it:

> Though the fig tree may not blossom,
> Nor fruit be on the vines;
> Though the labour of the olive may fail,
> And the fields yield no food;
> Though the flock be cut off from the fold,
> And there be no herd in the stalls—
> Yet I will rejoice in the Lord,
> I will joy in the God of my salvation.
> The Lord God is my strength;
> He will make my feet like deer's feet,
> And he will make me walk on my high hills.
>
> Habakkuk 3:18–19

Habakkuk too had discovered that God is worth loving and serving just for who he is.

In the examples of both Job and Habakkuk, we see an expression of trust. Trust is a confidence and a security in God. It recognizes his wisdom, that he knows best; his faithfulness, that he never changes, nor will he ever let us down; and his goodness, that he always wants what is best for his children. It rests in the fact that ultimately, whatever we face in life, God is on the throne and in control. Sometimes we will need to trust the Lord in situations where we cannot understand why he has allowed certain things to take place. I do not always understand why, but I do trust him!

Count your blessings

Trust is based on God's trust-worthiness, the fact that he is faithful and in the past has proved himself reliable and dependable. Sometimes I meet Christians who say, 'God does not answer my prayers.' However, as I have shown in chapter 5, were they to take a trip down Memory Lane, they would discover many past blessings received at God's hand. By reminding ourselves of God's faithfulness in the past, we assure ourselves of his faithfulness in the future.

When David was being pursued by those seeking to take his life, he said, 'Whenever I am afraid, I will trust in you' (Psalm 56:3). Even in the absence of a specific 'word' or God's intervention, David could say, 'I acknowledge God is going to do what is right.'

God wants the best for your life, more than you do! Trust holds on to God's promises, waiting patiently for his timing. A righteous man, 'shall not be afraid of evil tidings, his heart is fixed, trusting in the Lord' (Psalm 112:7, KJV).

Roll them on to the Rock—Christ Jesus

The primary Old Testament word for 'trust' is *galal*, which basically means to 'roll'. David used it when he said, 'Our fathers trusted in you; they *trusted*, and you delivered them. They cried to you, and were delivered; they *trusted* in you, and were not ashamed' (Psalm 22:4–5). The Bible promises that as we trust in the Lord with all our heart, not leaning on our own understanding, but acknowledging him in all our ways, he will direct our paths (Proverbs 3:5).

There is a tremendous security in being able to give a situation to the Lord and to trust him with it. It brings a peace that passes all understanding. While all those around us are panicking, we can stand firm, immovable, trusting in the Lord and in his faithfulness. 'Those who trust in the Lord are like Mount Zion, which cannot be moved, but abides for ever' (Psalm 125:1).

Why is it that people 'go under' in situations? Why is it that when pressure comes along people are crushed? It is because, as we have seen, *God did not make us to be weight-lifters!* He tells us to cast all our cares upon him—to roll them on him (1 Peter 5:7). Give the situation over to him. Raising hands is a universal way of saying 'I surrender'. Often when a situation is causing me concern I will lift my hands to the Lord as if I had that person or situation in them, saying, 'Over to you, Lord. I give this situation to you. I trust you with it and am not going to worry.'

Don't worry

The story is told of a man whose neighbour kept chickens. Among them was a cockerel, whose occasional crowing greatly bothered him. Early one morning, in despair, he phoned up its owner and complained, 'That miserable bird of yours keeps me awake all night.'

His neighbour replied, 'I don't understand, he makes hardly any noise at all. I don't think you will find that he crows more than a few times in an entire day.'

The angry man quickly replied, 'That isn't my problem. It's not how often he crows that disturbs me;

it's never knowing when he might crow that keeps me from sleeping.'

Have you noticed that many of the things which we worry about never actually come to pass? Often we become anxious, anticipating problems that might come. Jesus in his great wisdom exhorted us, 'Do not worry about tomorrow, for tomorrow will worry about its own things. Sufficient for the day is its own trouble' (Matthew 6:34). The Lord says, 'Don't worry', yet we often reply, 'But you don't understand, Lord.' If God says, 'Don't worry' there is no reason why you should worry. The Lord has promised that he will not allow us to be put under more pressure than we can cope with (1 Corinthians 10:13).

Although he does sometimes allow us to go through difficult experiences to throw us afresh on him and to develop our character, he says, 'Don't worry. Cast your cares on to me. I care. I can cope with that.' (See 1 Peter 5:7.) Yet we are tempted to battle away, trying to solve the problems ourselves. So often Christians worry about situations rather then heeding Paul's exhortation to 'Be anxious for nothing, but in everything by prayer and supplication, with thanksgiving, let your requests be made known to God; and the peace of God, which surpasses all understanding, will guard your hearts and minds through Christ Jesus' (Philippians 4:6–7). The knowledge that God is in control certainly does bring a peace which is beyond understanding.

We know who is on the throne and when those around us are being shaken by the problems of life, as Christians we can stand firm. The hymn writer put it:

O what peace we often forfeit,
O what needless pain we bear—
All because we do not carry
Everything to God in prayer!

Joseph Scriven

You can trust the Lord and say, 'The Lord is my helper; I will not fear. What can men do to me?' (Hebrews 13:6).

Having the right mental attitude towards life is so important. Experts tell us that worry is not something which originates from outside of us, for example in the things that are going on around. It is something which starts internally. It is not your job, your family, or your responsibilities which causes the worry, but your response to those things. That is why the Lord says, 'Do not worry. Cast your cares on me. Trust me. I am big enough to cope with that situation. You are not. You will go under.'

Jesus Christ is Lord

Another Hebrew word for 'trust' is *chasah*, which means, 'to flee to for refuge as to a rock, shield or some other protective thing'.

'He who dwells in the secret place of the Most High shall abide under the shadow of the Almighty. I will say of the Lord, "He is my refuge and my fortress; my God, in him I will trust" ' (Psalm 91:1–2).

Most of us have experienced the pain of seemingly unanswered prayer or the dilemma when our prayers have not been answered as quickly as we wanted them to be. It is in those situations that we really have to hold on in faith, trusting in the Lord. So often Christians declare, 'Jesus is Lord', and yet situations come along and throw them, causing them to panic and to become fearful. Then they start to talk negatively, which proves that they are not really convinced of Christ's lordship. The apostle Paul says, '*We know* that all things work together for good to those who love God, to those who are called according to his purpose' (Romans 8:28). Do we know or do we just hope that all things work together for good? God has an amazing ability to turn wicked men's intentions to our own good and Satan's attacks to the destruction of Satan's kingdom.

Have you ever considered the three Hebrew lads who were thrown into the fiery furnace for their love of the Lord? This was an example of God knowing best. I could imagine some of the observers saying, 'A God of love wouldn't allow such a thing to happen.' It was because he is a God of love that he allowed it. Listen to the words of those lads: 'Our God whom we serve is able to deliver us from the burning fiery furnace, and he will deliver us from your hand, O king. But if not, let it be known to you, O king, that we do not serve your gods, nor will we worship the gold image which you have set up' (Daniel 3:17–18). They could have missed the fiery furnace, but they would have also missed the presence of the One 'like the Son of God' and the king having a change of heart.

Jesus, freshly empowered by the Holy Spirit, was not led by the Spirit to the nearest pulpit, but was driven out into the wilderness to be tempted forty days by the devil (Matthew 4:1). Often such trials and testings are an important part of our equipping and our training. When our faith is tried, we can get bitter or better. We can blame God, or get to know his love more deeply.

Visualize Paul and Silas as they are imprisoned in a dungeon with their feet in stocks and their backs bleeding. What are they doing? Are they complaining? Are they saying, 'Lord, we expected you to get us out of here. How come you sent an angel to release Peter from prison but you didn't send one for us?' No, they are praising God, even at midnight! How can they praise God in such circumstances? Because they realize that he is on the throne. They could have missed the prison, the bleeding backs and the stocks, but they would also have missed the jailer and his whole family being saved (Acts 16:16–34)!

Someone once put it—'*God has a brilliant and wonderful way of disguising opportunities so that they look like problems*!'

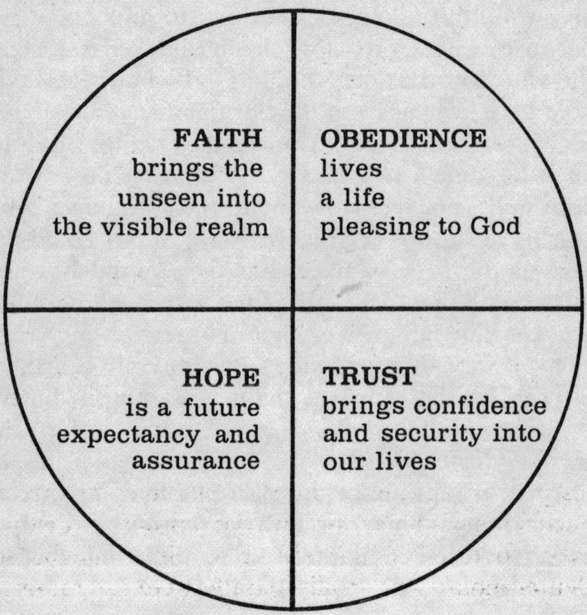

Trust, along with faith, hope and obedience, are complementary and all vital to the balanced life of the believer. They are different, yet, each a part of the whole. (See diagram.)

1. *Faith* brings the unseen into the visible realm.
2. We will consider in chapter 14 the importance of *obedience*, of living a life of faith that is pleasing to God.
3. *Hope* is a future expectancy, future faith, the assurance of Christ's return and our eternal home in glory.
4. *Trust* brings confidence and security whatever we may experience in life.

God does not promise a problem-free life, but we are called to be overcomers. How can we be overcomers, if we never have any problems to overcome? What God does promise us is that we can come out of every situation victorious. Let us consider five purposes for the trials we go through.

1. Trials reveal wrong attitudes

Often we do not recognize our wrong attitudes until we are put under pressure. It has been said, 'If you squeeze an orange, orange juice comes out.' What happens when you are squeezed?

Many try to blame someone else for their reactions. They complain: 'They made me react that way!' But, in reality, people cannot 'make' you react. All they do is reveal what is inside you, so that you can get it dealt with by the Lord.

2. Trials mature us

They deal with instabilities in our lives. Sometimes God in his wisdom takes away any props that we may have, to throw us afresh on to him. The book of Deuteronomy beautifully parallels God's training of the saint with how a mother eagle teaches her baby to fly: 'As an eagle stirs up its nest. Hovers over its young, spreading out its wings, taking them up. Carrying them on its wings, so the Lord alone led him' (Deuteronomy 32:11–12).

Visualize the baby eagle, snuggled up in the comfort of his nest, thinking how wonderful life is. It's another new day and mother eagle has just returned with more delicious food for Junior. As he observes other eagles flying overhead, his conclusion is, 'You'll never see me in one of those!'

He is totally oblivious of the fact that it is his destiny to fly!

However, as the days pass by, mother decides that it is time for baby's first flying lesson. To give him some incentive, she removes the soft comfortable down from the nest, leaving bare twigs. Now Junior is beginning to think that maybe flying is not such a bad idea. So when mother says,'Would you like to go for a ride on my back?' Junior is very eager. He climbs up and clings on tightly as mother soars into the sky. Soon he is beginning to find the experience quite exhilarating, waves a baby eagle wing and shouts to other nest-bound eagles, 'I bet you wish you had a private jet!'

Suddenly mother dives, leaving baby eagle in the air, like a Walt Disney cartoon character who has just realized he has walked off the edge of a cliff! Junior begins to descend, flapping frantically, to no avail. Just before he hits the ground, mother swoops underneath, catching him on her back and flies into the sky again.

Junior clings on tightly, his baby eagle heart beating rapidly as he says, 'Mother, I thought you loved me! What a horrible thing to do. Please don't ever do that again.'

But, it is too late—mother has disappeared once more. Again baby flaps and flaps as he descends, until mother repeats the process, catching him on her back and transporting him upwards. However, each time baby eagle's wings are becoming stronger, until on one occasion as baby frantically flaps, he finds he is no longer descending. 'I can fly!' he exclaims.

Do you see the similarities to when we first were saved? Life seemed so easy. It was as though we had experienced an end to all problems as we lay back in the security and comfort of our new nest. However, God wants us to be victorious, soaring Christians, not nest-bound babies. Eventually he decides 'It's time for you to learn to fly', and flying is something which the text books cannot teach you. Some lessons we learn only through the experiences of life, which can be painful. It has been said that 'Real growth in grace is the result of sanctified trials.'

3. Trials teach us to withstand Satan

The Bible tells us 'We do not wrestle against flesh and blood, but against principalities, against powers, against the rulers of the darkness of this age' (Ephesians 6:12). We are involved in a spiritual war, yet so many Christians passively accept every attack and sickness that the devil throws at them. Satan is out to kill you, to steal from you and to destroy you (John 10:10). Nevertheless, by the prayer of faith we can see in our lives Christ's victory over sin, sickness and Satan's power. (I cover this subject in greater depth in my earlier book *Battle Stations*, Kingsway Publications 1984.)

4. Trials throw us afresh on the Lord

Sometimes trials are a prod to prayer. When all is going well, we can be tempted to forget how dependent we are on the Lord. The story is told of a person who had a vision of his whole life as two sets of footsteps in the sand, the Lord's and his own. During the trials of life, he saw just one set of footsteps and said, 'Lord, where were you when I was going through those trials? Why was there only one set of footprints? Where were you when I needed you most?'

The Lord replied, 'Those were the times that I carried you.'

We may feel we are alone, but God's 'everlasting arms' are in fact never far away.

5. Trials can also develop real friendships

When trials come, we have two possible courses of action:

(a) We can try to look spiritual and pretend that there is no problem. We can hide what is really going on inside. This will drive us away from other Christians.

(b) Trials can bring us close to fellow believers. The people that I am closest to today are those with whom I have shared openly when I have been going through real problems and trials. The Bible tells us to bear one another's burdens and to weep with those who weep. But how can I bear your burdens if I do not know that you have any? How can I weep with you, if you always weep alone? We are called to stand together. I praise God for the friends that he has given me, for the people I can go to at any time and share anything with, knowing that they love me and that they will pray and stand with me.

So you see that trials can mature us, and teach us to trust the Lord.

PART TWO

Hindrances to Answered Prayer

11

Lord, Teach Us to Pray

When you pray, do not use vain repetitions as the heathen do. For they think that they will be heard for their many words. Therefore do not be like them. For your Father knows the things you have need of before you ask him. In this manner, therefore, pray:

> Our Father in heaven,
> Hallowed be your name,
> Your kingdom come,
> Your will be done
> On earth as it is in heaven.
> Give us this day our daily bread.
> And forgive us our debts,
> As we forgive our debtors.
> And do not lead us into temptation,
> But deliver us from the evil one,
> For yours is the kingdom and the power and the glory
> for ever.
> Amen.

Matthew 6:7–13

We have considered in some depth that our prayers are supposed to be answered and we saw in chapter 5 that Christians have no right to dismiss any apparent failure of their prayers with the words, 'Well, it obviously was not the Lord's will.'

We have seen that the main cause of unanswered prayer is unbelief. Now let us look at seven other common hindrances to answered prayer. As you read, allow the Holy Spirit to search your heart and deal with any blockages that may become evident.

The apostle James made it clear to the Christians to whom he was writing that the basic reason why they failed to receive God's blessing was 'because you do not ask . . .' (James 4:2). Apathy is a major reason why people do not see answered prayer. Notice, when teaching on prayer, Jesus did not say, 'if you pray' but 'when you pray' (Matthew 6:7).

After explaining the obvious reason why people do not experience answered prayer, James went on to give a further reason, 'You ask and do not receive, because you ask amiss' (James 4:3). Just as a broken electrical cable can prevent my car from functioning properly, so wrong attitudes and broken lines of communication with God can prevent my prayers being answered in the way God intends them to be.

In teaching his disciples to pray, Jesus gave them a framework or an outline for effective praying. He told them to pray 'in this manner', not to mechanically rattle off the prayer each week. As Spurgeon put it, 'to recite the Lord's prayer and believe that you have prayed is the height of foolishness.'

Therefore, in pursuing our goal of an effective prayer life, we do well to follow Jesus' guidelines. For this reason, I have taken seven sections of what has commonly been called 'the Lord's Prayer' and considered the opposite of each section. These are as follows:

1. A wrong concept of God
2. Unholiness
3. Selfishness
4. A fear of asking
5. Resentment
6. Guilt
7. Presumption

12

A Wrong Concept of God

When you pray, you shall not be like the hypocrites. For they love to pray standing in the synagogues and on the corners of the streets, that they may be seen by men. Assuredly, I say to you, they have their reward. But you, when you pray, go into your room, and when you have shut your door, pray to your Father, who is in the secret place; and your Father who sees in secret will reward you openly. But when you pray, do not use vain repetitions as the heathen do. For they think that they will be heard for their many words. Therefore do not be like them. For your Father knows the things you have need of before you ask him. In this manner, therefore, pray: Our Father in heaven.

Matthew 6:5–9

We cannot reach higher in prayer than our concept of God. If we regard God as some austere being afar off, we will never be able to approach him confidently in prayer. Notice at the beginning of Jesus' discourse on prayer, he reveals God as a family God, one who is our 'Father'. Such a concept would have been regarded as blasphemous by the Jews. They would not even have spoken the name 'God' (Yahweh), let alone called him

'Father'. Encouraging such intimacy in prayer did not make Jesus popular. Notice though, that it was always the religious people Jesus was upsetting! It was the sinners, the tax collectors, the prostitutes and those who were despised in society, who were attracted to him, for they saw in him relevant answers to the problems they faced in life. Jesus came to introduce them to God and to bring them into a personal relationship with him.

In a very real sense, God is not his name but his job. Father is the name by which Jesus reveals God to us. So many in prayer speak to God as though he were some distant being, rather than 'our Father'. God wants us to progress from a business relationship to the intimacy of family. Jesus came to reveal God's paternal love for us. Imagine my earthly father's reaction were I to greet him with the words, 'O thou blessed contracting electrician.' Although my statement would be true and describes his job, to me his name is 'Dad'.

> For as many as are led by the Spirit of God, these are sons of God. For you did not receive a spirit of bondage again to fear, but you received the Spirit of adoption by whom we cry out, 'Abba, Father.' The Spirit himself bears witness with our spirit that we are children of God, and if children, then heirs—heirs of God and joint heirs with Christ.
> Romans 8:14–17

Our cry is 'Abba, Father'. The literal Aramaic translation of the word 'Abba' is 'Daddy', not even the mature paternal word 'Father'. 'Abba' would be among the first words learnt by the Hebrew child.

I believe that the Lord wants to restore to us childlike simplicity in prayer. Jesus teaches us that we are 'not to use vain repetition', nor will we be 'heard' for our many words. Putting on an unnatural or high-pitched voice or even speaking in sixteenth century English may be a religious tradition. However, it is not helpful in encouraging people to develop a natural walk with God, nor is it a sign of spirituality. It is interesting to notice that from all the languages, including certain religious languages that were available, the Lord arranged that the New Testament should be written originally in Koine Greek, the common language of everyday people. It is to these folk that he brought the good news.

However much we may like the beauty of sixteenth century English, it will never reach twentieth century man! God wants us to be ourselves when we pray.

Hands together, eyes closed

Even the childhood concept of praying with our 'hands together and eyes closed' is unhelpful. Although it may at times be an aid to concentration, it further increases the feeling of unnaturalness. We do not have to approach God with our heads bowed, like a naughty child approaching his father, who has just discovered his misdeeds. We can look the Lord straight in the eyes, knowing that we are forgiven. When Jesus prayed, rather than bowing his head, he 'lifted up his eyes to heaven' (John 17:1). David said, 'I will lift up my eyes to the hills—where does my help come from? My help comes from the Lord, the Maker of heaven and earth' (Psalm 121:1–2, NIV).

No special posture or language is required in prayer. Rather, God wants us to relax and enjoy a natural love relationship with him. He is interested in every area of our lives. There should be no 'secular' and 'sacred' divide in the Christian life.

There is no area of our life which we should hold back from the Lord. There is a great release in pouring our heart out to God. Whatever you share, he won't be shocked. He knows how you feel anyway. 'All things are naked and open to the eyes of him to whom we must give an account' (Hebrews 4:13). 'We do not have a high priest who cannot sympathize with our weaknesses, but was in all points tempted as we are, yet without sin. Let us therefore come boldly to the throne of grace, that we may obtain mercy and find grace to help in time of need' (Hebrews 4:15–16). Any area that we have been tempted in, the Lord was tempted in too.

God is your Father. He loves you so much. He could never love you any more than he does now! Did you realize that he loves you as much as he loves Jesus? Jesus said, 'You have loved them as you have loved me' (John 17:23). Isn't it wonderful to know that we are loved so much! We are each unique and special to the Lord. He has 'called you by name' (Isaiah 43:1).

God is '*our Father*', one to whom no problem is too small and insignificant. And he is 'our Father *in heaven*', to whom no problem is too big! So many Christians are held back from having a loving and relaxed relationship with their heavenly Father because they have never enjoyed a loving relaxed relationship with an earthly father. The Lord wants to come and heal those hurts and set his children free so that they can enjoy communion with him.

Walking with God

We read that, 'Enoch walked with God; and he was not, for God took him' (Genesis 5:24). Enoch knew what it was to enjoy continual, unbroken fellowship with the Lord. One little girl, recounting the story to her Sunday School class, beautifully illustrated this point by saying, 'The Lord went for a walk with Enoch. They walked and they talked, and they talked and they walked. Then the Lord said to Enoch, "We have come so far now, it is not worth you going home, you may as well come home with me."'

'We come into your presence'

The statement, 'Lord, we come into your presence', has unfortunately become a common one in Christian circles. In reality it is a very strange thing to pray, as there is no way of getting out of his presence. Although we may not always be aware of God's presence, we cannot escape it. He has promised never to leave us, nor forsake us, but always to be with us. It is an unscriptural concept to associate church buildings with the presence of God. God does not dwell in buildings made with hands. We are the temple of the Holy Spirit, 'the Lord's house'. In reality, we are as much in God's presence in our car or in the bath as in a religious building. It appears that Jesus found the hills more conducive to prayer than any religious building of his day. We cannot get out of God's presence.

It is an awesome thing to realize that we even sin in God's presence!

We live in God's presence and therefore it does not matter where we are, our prayers can still be heard.

Daniel prayed from his room. Jesus prayed from a garden. Paul prayed while bound between guards in prison and Jonah prayed from the belly of a large fish! It is out of this realization that we can cultivate an intimate continual walk with the Lord.

I very much enjoy going for a walk along the cliff tops or through a field, chatting with the Lord. On occasions I have been driving to a meeting in my car with tears running down my face, just expressing my gratitude to the Lord for the opportunity of being entrusted with his word. It is perfectly natural to communicate silently with the Lord throughout the day, in every situation. Sometimes, I will look up smiling and say things like, 'Help, Lord', or, 'Over to you, Lord'. I love to find things for which to express gratitude to him. We simply enjoy each other's company.

Prayer is not just making requests; it is communicating with the Lord. Jesus exhorted us always to pray (Luke 18:1) and the Bible tells us to pray without ceasing (1 Thessalonians 5:17). Prayer should be the most natural thing for the Christian. This obviously does not mean that we should walk around with our eyes closed, but be continuously in an attitude of prayer, in fellowship with the Father, every minute of every hour of every day. The hymn writer put it beautifully:

> He walks with me and He talks with me,
> And tells me I am His own.
> And the joy we share as we tarry there,
> None other has ever known.

Does he walk with you and talk with you? If so, what

was your last conversation about?

Could you imagine a couple whose only communication was fifteen minutes a day scrupulously set aside to talk together? Could you imagine them stopping the conversation with the words, 'Sorry, time up. See you again tomorrow, same time, same place!' I am not discouraging set times with the Lord; they are very scriptural (Daniel 6:10; Psalms 5:3, 55:17). However, our devotional life should be far more than just that!

Soon after my conversion, I heard teaching on tithing and assumed that it affected every area of my life and that I should tithe my time in order to pray. So, as a new Christian, I set aside two hours and twenty-four minutes a day for prayer! The first few minutes were fine, but soon I ran out of things to say and on a number of occasions fell asleep and woke up feeling more guilty than ever. The last few moments of my prayer vigil brightened up as I anticipated the forthcoming reward of a relaxed evening. Although my actions were sincere, my prayer life was not motivated by a living relationship with the Lord, but by legalism. For unless love is the motive, quiet times will be boring and will usually not last for very long. God does not want the times we spend with him to be an endurance test! I discovered that it was better to set aside fifteen minutes to half an hour, when I could really use the time to the maximum and soon found that it was not long enough. These days, it is not uncommon for me to spend a couple of hours or more alone with the Lord. However, my motive for doing so is not a sense of obligation, but because I love him and enjoy his company. I love at the end of the day to fall asleep talking with the Lord. Many Christians have felt guilty about falling asleep when praying. However, what could be more beautiful than a child who falls asleep talking with his father, who then tucks him in?

If you find it hard to sleep at night, don't count sheep, talk to the Shepherd!

13

Unholiness

'Hallowed be thy name'

During a recent ministry trip, I had to share a room with another Christian. Waking up the next morning I said, 'John, I had a dream last night.' He looked at me, intrigued to hear more, so I continued, 'It was nothing spiritual. I just saved the world. You know like James Bond.'

With a smile on his face, he retorted, 'Oh, only James Bond? I like a person with a balanced self-image.' With that we began to laugh together. James Bond does not have a balanced self image. Both his lifestyle and his ability to come out of every situation unruffled are unreal. However, this started me thinking about how much we need a 'balanced God image', or 'God revelation'.

In the opening lines of the Lord's Prayer, Jesus not only reveals God as our Father but also as one who is 'hallowed' or 'holy'. Our intimacy with God must never lead to disrespect or flippancy. God is not a 'heavenly fairy-Godmother' to get us out of tight spots. He is King, seated on the throne, one whose kingdom is going to come in power and nothing will stop it! Do we have a balanced God revelation? The only fear permissible for the Christian is the fear of the Lord, that is, a healthy respect for who God is.

Many Christians' prayers are nullified by their life-style. The answer to the psalmist's question, 'Who may ascend into the hill of the Lord? Or who may stand in his holy place?' is clear: 'He who has clean hands and a pure heart' (Psalm 24:3–4).

It is sin which causes a separation between us and God. We are warned in Psalm 66:18 that if we regard iniquity in our heart, the Lord will not hear. As a result of his sin, King David lost his child. Despite his lying on the ground, pleading and crying to God, his prayer was not answered. So many Christians approach God trying to justify their actions and to prove that they are right, thus failing to hear anything God may be wanting to say to them.

I recently received a telephone call from a woman who was distressed at her friend's illness and kept saying, 'Why is God allowing it?' The woman was resentful against the Lord. Knowing something of the situation, I shared areas where scriptural principles in the sick woman's life were being violated.

The woman instantly rejected my counsel, and continued to ask the same question, 'Why is God allowing it?' I called in one of my colleagues, who knew nothing of the situation, and handed the phone over to him. After he had talked with the woman a few moments, he gave her the same advice. But once again she instantly rejected it, because it was not what she wanted to hear. She put the phone down, still blaming God and asking why he was allowing it, refusing to hear the clear answer from God's word.

Many Christians disobey God's word, then blame him for the results. Many of the pressures we experience are self-inflicted. When we deliberately sin, we come out from underneath God's covering. While a person is in submission to God, he is under his protective umbrella. However, if he comes out from underneath that umbrella, he can blame no one but himself if he gets wet! The sincerity of our love for the Lord is not demonstrated by the words we speak or sing, but by our lifestyle. He says, 'If you love me, keep my commandments' (John 14:15).

Many Christians meet together to pray on Sunday yet live the other six days in a way that drags God's name into the ground. Their behaviour and attitudes nullify their witness and turn their friends, colleagues and family away from the Lord. Paul said to the Jews, 'The name of God is blasphemed among the Gentiles because of you' (Romans 2:24). Such an accusation brings an awesome responsibility.

'If you do, I will...'

A few years back 'promise boxes' were popular. Each day a card with one of God's promises on could be pulled out to be claimed. However, many of these promise boxes were biased, frequently just containing the positive promises and even missing out the conditions. Most of God's promises are conditional. In other words, 'If you do this, I will do this. If you do not do this, I will do this.' We are told that 'whatever we ask, we receive from him...' (1 John 3:22). But the reason for our receiving whatever we ask is given: 'because we keep his commandments and do those things that are pleasing in his sight.'

For example, God promises that he will 'open for you the windows of heaven and pour out for you such blessing that there will not be room enough to receive it', and that he will 'rebuke the devourer for your sakes, so that he will not destroy the fruit of your ground, nor shall the vine fail to bear fruit for you in the field', and 'all nations will call you blessed, for you will be a delightful land'. But this promise is conditional on the fact that we 'bring all the tithes into the storehouse' (Malachi 3:10–12). Not only does he promise abundance to those who honour him in their finances, but he also says, 'You are cursed with a curse, for you have robbed me' (Malachi 3:9). God will not bless disobedience.

Whoever heard of a 'promise box' containing such scriptures as, 'If you forsake the Lord and serve foreign gods, then he will turn and do you harm and consume you, after he has done you good' (Joshua 24:20? However, it is still a promise from God's word! When claiming God's promises, it is well worth considering any conditions attached to the blessing, and the context that the scripture is written in.

Some Christians try to move in faith, while living in disobedience to God. Therefore, their faith is nullified. Sadly, many men of faith in the past have gone off the rails because godliness has been a missing ingredient in their life. Other Christians live in obedience to the Scriptures, but as there is no flow of faith their Christian life is lifeless and boring.

Faith and obedience are complementary. Obedience should always be the result of God speaking. When God said, 'Let there be light', there was light! (Genesis 1:3) Abel, by faith, offered a sacrifice acceptable to God in obedience (Hebrews 11:4). Enoch's testimony was that, 'he pleased God' (Hebrews 11:5). Noah, 'became heir of the righteousness which is according to faith' (Hebrews 11:7) by obeying God and building an ark in which his whole household was saved! Imagine building a boat in the desert! No doubt Noah's obedience caused much persecution and ridicule. But *the things which we do demonstrate what we believe.* 'Someone will say, "You have faith and I have works." Show me your faith without your works, and I will show you my faith by my works' (James 2:18).

> *By faith Abraham obeyed* when he was called to go out to the place which he would afterwards receive as an inheritance. And he went out, not knowing where he was going. By faith he sojourned in the land of promise as in a foreign country, dwelling in tents with Isaac and Jacob, the heirs with him of the same promise; for he waited for the city which has foundations, whose builder and maker is God.
>
> Hebrews 11:8–10

Some of Jesus' commands were very unorthodox and unusual. Take, for example, his sending his disciples to collect the donkey for his entry into Jerusalem. I wonder if thoughts of the penalty for donkey stealing crossed their minds as they went? His instruction for them simply to inform the owner, should he ask, that 'the Lord has need of him', probably brought little comfort to them! After all, would you willingly stand by and let your donkey go in such circumstances?

Fishing for your tax money is a somewhat unusual occupation too. Try explaining to the waiting tax man where you are going with your fishing rod. Imagine replying to a fellow angler who asks which type of fish you are after, 'One with money in its mouth'! Yet obedience always brings blessing. We never lose out by obeying God. However, disobedience and unholiness will rob us of the joys and blessing of answered prayer. 'For the eyes of the Lord are on the righteous, and his ears are open to their prayers; but the face of the Lord is against those who do evil' (1 Peter 3:12).

14

Selfishness

'Your kingdom come, your will be done as it is in heaven'

Earlier in this book, we saw that God does not call us to a passive acceptance of our circumstances, but to pray actively for his kingdom rule to be established and his will to be done on earth. We have the assurance that, in this world marred by sin, one day we will see Christ's total rule. Until then, we can progressively see Satan, sin and the flesh dethroned and the rightful King enthroned. As we have considered in the previous chapter, this dethroning needs to take place first in our own hearts and lives. This section of the Lord's Prayer searches the hidden motives of our heart. So much prayer is motivated by selfishness.

The travail of his soul

It is not selfish to claim the promises of God, rather he invites us to do so. The Scriptures tell us that 'He shall see the travail of his soul, and be satisfied' (Isaiah

53:11). Many Christians say such things as, 'I won't ask the Lord to heal me, I wouldn't want to use him.'

'I do not know whether to come to the Lord with my financial need, because I do not want to use God.'

'I feel hurt inside but I do not want God to feel I am using him by asking him to heal me.'

Such statements demonstrate that we have failed to realize that when Christ died, he was dying on our behalf, as our substitute. He was bearing our sin, our sickness, our poverty and our hurts and rejection. He was bearing them so that we do not have to. Consequently, when we come to him to receive healing, he sees 'the travail of his soul, and is satisfied'. In other words, he says, 'Bearing their sicknesses was worthwhile.' When someone is saved he sees 'the travail of his soul, and is satisfied'. They were worth dying for! He longs for you to receive his salvation, healing and wholeness.

He wants you to enjoy your inheritance. For example, imagine someone spending all his money to buy you a gift. If you took the present and really appreciated it, he would feel fulfilled. Although it had been very costly to purchase, he would feel that it had been worthwhile. However, if you walked off saying, 'No, you keep it; I wouldn't want to use you', do you think that would please him? No, it was a waste of his money. It is not selfish to receive our inheritance! I want the Lord to see the travail of his soul and be satisfied.

Right motives

However, sometimes our motives for wanting to receive are at the expense of others. An example is when James and John's mother came to Jesus, with the request that her sons be given the top positions in his kingdom. If her prayer had been answered it would have been at the expense of others. In my life and ministry I long to be all that God wants me to be and for him to use me mightily. However, I do not want my desire to stand in the way of him using others. If there was someone more anointed to minister on a certain occasion, I would have no problems stepping down, for my desire is to see his kingdom come and his will done, not my kingdom come and my will done.

There have been occasions when I have prayed, knowing that were my prayer to be instantly answered, I would be admired. Sometimes, on such occasions, the Lord has allowed things to go in the opposite direction. Then, when I have been at rock bottom, realizing that I am totally dependent on him, the prayer has been answered. Do we pray that God might be glorified or that we might be admired? Selfishness and pride can greatly hinder our praying.

Jesus' guide to prayer begins by requesting that God might be hallowed, his kingdom might come and his will might be done on earth, as in heaven. Right at the start, the goal of our praying is that the Lord might be glorified. Satan's temptations to Jesus were to use God for his own convenience and glory. However, Jesus resisted them for 'Christ did not please himself' (Romans 15:3). So often wrong attitudes can spoil good prayers. Is my ultimate goal in prayer that I might serve the Lord more effectively or that he might serve me? When we pray, 'Hallowed be thy name', we are adding a safety clause and permitting God to overrule our prayer if we are praying amiss.

It has often been said that God's answer to prayer is

sometimes 'Yes', sometimes 'No', and on other occasions 'Wait'. Looking back, I am so glad that the Lord did not always say 'Yes' to my prayers. Because of our limited knowledge, we can sometimes ask for things that are not good for us. It is when God says 'No', or 'Wait, you are not ready yet', that we really need to trust him.

Monica, the mother of Augustine, one of the early church leaders, pleaded with the Lord to stop her son leaving home and going to Rome. It seemed that the Lord ignored her prayer, yet through that journey her son was converted. What she felt was God's failure to answer her prayer, in fact transcended all of her desires. Though he denied her heartcry, she did not lose out. His answer was far greater.

Augustine later commented, 'Thou in Thy hidden wisdom, didst grant the substance of her desire. Ye refused the things she prayed for, in order that Thou mightest effect in me what she was ever praying for. She loved to keep me with her, as mothers are wont, yes, far more than most mothers, and she knew not what joy thou wast preparing for her out of my desertion!'

Your will be done

In the garden of Gethsemane, when Jesus was faced with the ultimate sacrifice, he prayed, 'Father, if it is your will, remove this cup from me; nevertheless not my will, but yours, be done.' It was in that situation that 'an angel appeared to him from heaven, strengthening him' (Luke 22:42–43). Prayer is not wrestling to get my own way. *May we, like Jesus, make sure that our only motivation in life is to be a 'Father pleaser'.*

We need to see that God loves us and wants us to njoy fully our inheritance, but not to the extent of sing others. This is a common mistake made by those eeking a partner. Many have come from broken omes and are longing for security. Seeking the satis-action of their emotional needs, they go looking for a artner. When their request is delayed or denied, ather than searching their heart and seeking advice, o see if there is a reason for the delay, many complain nd doubt God's sincerity in promising to answer all heir prayers. However, as we have seen, God will not less us at the expense of others. What kind of marriage artner would someone be who sought only their own motional satisfaction? First, they need to come and eceive healing for the hurts in their lives, that they night enter a relationship to give, not just to receive.

Others seek for a husband or wife as a status-symbol r even as someone to do the practical jobs around the ouse! Again, no wonder their prayers go unanswered. This point is amusingly illustrated by a young lady, who in every church prayer meeting prayed for a usband. One day, out of exasperation, her elders pproached her and forbade her to pray publicly for a usband any more. At the next prayer meeting she tood and prayed, 'Lord, give my mother and father a on-in-law.' I am certainly not suggesting that it is vrong for a person to pray for a partner, merely that ur attitudes and motivation must be right. If someone loes not feel a natural love growing in their heart for ou, it is no use praying for God to give that person to ou as a partner. I have met many misguided Chris-ians, who say such things as, 'The Lord has told me hat I am to marry that person, but they are rebelling gainst his will.' Any future relationship, if it is to work, must be entered into willingly and whole heartedly by both partners.

Some Christians are so untidy, frumpish and care less in the area of personal hygiene, that God migh have a job convincing any potential partner of hi choice!

Many who are praying for their unsaved partner tc get saved are doing so purely for their own con venience, rather than for their partner's eterna benefit. Some would do well to pray more that Goc will make them a better husband or wife and deal witl selfishness, untidiness, lack of consideration, unrealit or unsubmissiveness in their own lives. God's king dom rule must first begin in us. If we are unwilling tc surrender all to Jesus, how can we expect answers tc our prayers for others to allow Jesus to be Lord in thei lives? Maybe some parents will need to deal witl unreality in their own Christian lives and ask thei children's forgiveness for any hypocrisy, before they see change in them too. 'You ask and do not receive because you ask amiss, that you may spend it on you pleasures' (James 4:3).

15

A Fear of Asking

'Give us this day our daily bread'

An outright request for God's provision might seem out of place in such a God-centred introduction to prayer. However, asking is no less spiritual than praising. God delights to give to his children! Even when we were lost, with no other hope, 'God so loved the world that he *gave* his only begotten Son, that whoever believes in him should not perish but have everlasting life' (John 3:16). All that we have, all that we are and all that we will ever be, is dependent on him. When our attitudes are right, we can come boldly and ask.

The idea that we should only pray for other people's needs and not our own is also a misunderstanding of prayer. God wants the best for us. When we are praying according to God's promises, we need have no fear about making requests. 'He who did not spare his own Son, but delivered him up for us all, how shall he not with him also freely give us *all* things?' (Romans 8:32)

Notice that the request is for God to give us 'our daily bread'. It is a prayer for material provision! So many Christians think that God is not interested in such mundane things. But he is interested in every area of our lives. As we have already said, there is no 'secular' and 'sacred' divide in the kingdom of God. God promises us in his word that, as we seek first his kingdom and righteousness, all the things we need shall be provided (Matthew 6:33). Some Christians mistakenly think that poverty is a mark of godliness and humility. The Scriptures, though, are abundantly clear that poverty is a curse. What reflection is it upon our heavenly father if his children live in need? If your children were walking around in rags, it would certainly reflect badly on your parental care.

God has committed himself to supplying, 'all your needs according to his riches in glory by Christ Jesus' (Philippians 4:19). It is out of his inexhaustible riches that he meets our needs, and we have a big God. I love the way the Living Bible puts the opening verse of Psalm 23: 'Because the Lord is my Shepherd, I have everything I need.' Let us therefore come boldly and without fear when we make our requests to him.

Notice, too, that the prayer is for daily 'bread'. The request is specific. We too need to be specific when we pray. Prior to his departure from them, Jesus said to his disciples, 'Until now you have asked nothing in my name. Ask, and you will receive, *that your joy may be full*' (John 16:24). Not only does the Lord find fulfilment in answering our prayers, but we too can find tremendous joy from seeing God meet our needs. If you analyse some prayers you hear you find that they sound good, but have no specific content. 'If you then, being evil, know how to give good gifts to your children, how much more will your Father who is in heaven give good things to those who *ask him*?' (Matthew 7:11).

16

Resentment

'Forgive us our debts, as we forgive our debtors'

Have you ever considered the implications of these words? It is like praying, 'Father, if I won't forgive others, don't forgive me.' Jesus went on to say, 'For if you forgive men their trespasses, your heavenly Father will also forgive you. But if you do not forgive men their trespasses, neither will your Father forgive your trespasses' (Matthew 6:14–15). A man once went to John Wesley to discuss someone who had offended him and said, 'I will never forgive', to which John Wesley replied, 'Then pray you never sin!'

It is so easy for disagreements, problems, unkind words, a simple misunderstanding or a feeling of being overlooked or misrepresented, to lead to resentment. Resentment is such a destructive thing. Not only does it destroy relationships, but it can destroy a person spiritually, so that they cannot relax and enjoy the Lord. It can stifle their Christian growth. Dr Paul Tournier said, 'Of all the things that choke and poison spiritual growth, resentment is probably the most devastatingly effective.' Many of God's children are not experiencing answered prayer and have lost the peace of God because of harbouring resentment in their heart.

Resentment can destroy a person emotionally too, leading to depression and tension. It can also destroy a person physically. A leading G.P. said, '80% of all my patients are suffering from physical diseases, the direct result of such things as fear, anxiety, anger and resentment.'

During one of our crusades, a woman in her mid-thirties came forward for prayer. She was bent double and crippled with arthritis. As I went to pray with her, the Lord said, 'Ask her who she resents.'

'Who is it you resent?' I enquired.

She went quiet and then burst into tears. A friend who had helped her forward said, 'Go on, tell him.'

She spoke the man's name and I explained how vital it was that she forgave him if she wanted to experience God's forgiveness, peace and healing. I encouraged her to speak out forgiveness. After a pause, she said the man's name as though he were there, adding, 'I forgive you.'

I never had to pray for her to be healed. When the root of bitterness in her heart was dealt with, God instantly healed her and she stood up straight and was able to move freely with no trace of arthritis left.

The root cause

Much depression is caused because people have not got their own way, either with God or with their partner, children, friends or minister. Often, the answer is not to be prayed with to be set free from the depression, but to repent of any resentment or sulking. When someone hurts us or fails to meet our expectations, it is then that we are faced with a choice, whether we will obey the scriptural command to forgive, or whether we will hold on to the hurt and pamper it, building up a mental file on the person who has hurt us, which we can later use to hurt them in revenge.

It is amazing how when we resent someone, we always feel justified. We feel that they 'deserve' our anger. We try to justify our feelings of resentment, saying such things as, 'I have a right to...', or, 'It was his fault...', for it is so easy to see other people's faults, isn't it? However, there is never a time when we do not have to forgive. Resentment is sin and if we regard iniquity in our hearts God will not hear us (Psalm 66:18). We have been forgiven such a great debt, one which we could never have paid off, and we are called to forgive as we have been forgiven. Each time we have to forgive, we are just reminded how much we have been forgiven!

Nine pence debts

Jesus told the story of a man who was forgiven a great debt, something in the region of five million pounds in today's currency! However, that same man left and found a servant who owed him nine pence and had the man imprisoned until he repaid the debt! (Matthew 18:21–30) This may sound absurd, but, Jesus then reflected on the Father's anger when we hold nine pence debts against one another after having been forgiven so much. Jesus gave his life, his all for you! When you consider the amount you have been forgiven, in comparison with the offence of the one who has wronged you, it is minute!

> Therefore, as the elect of God, holy and beloved, put on tender mercies, kindness, humbleness of mind, meekness,

> long-suffering; bearing with one another, and forgiving one another, if anyone has a complaint against another; *even as Christ forgave you, so you also must do.*
>
> Colossians 3:12–13

From the cross, Jesus prayed, 'Father, forgive them, for they do not know what they do' (Luke 23:34). So often those who hurt us do not realize what they have done. Many friendships have been broken with the alienated person still unaware of the reason for the rebuffs they have received.

Some Christians say, 'I would forgive him, if he asked me to.' However, we are called to forgive, whether or not the person asks for our forgiveness. As Stephen was martyred for his Christian testimony, he prayed, 'Lord, do not charge them with this sin' (Acts 7:60). In other words, 'Lord, I will pay this one. Do not put it on their bill!' Stephen did not even want God to take revenge on them! He chose to forgive. Have you?

Take a few moments to review your relationships and to see if there are any areas of resentment. It may be a member of your family: your parents, in-laws, a wayward child, an unfaithful partner, or an ex-boyfriend or girlfriend. Many people resent God because of the way they look or because they lost a loved one. In other cases the root is the break up of a relationship. Some people resent themselves because they have not reached their own goals and ambitions for their lives. Many Christians still hold resentment against a business partner who used them, a teacher who did not like them, a fellow employee, a neighbour, a minister or another denomination or church leader in their town. It may be another brother or sister in the Lord, someone whom God has blessed in a way you wish that he had blessed you. It could be a thief who broke into your home or attacked you. *Whoever it is, we are called to forgive.*

1. Repent of the resentment

See it is sin, and that there is ultimately no excuse.

2. Choose to forgive

Forgiving is a decision. It is something we choose to do. Usually our feelings and emotions follow later. We may not feel like forgiving but we can choose to forgive and then never again bring up the subject or criticize the one we have forgiven.

3. Seek to be reconciled

Now, let the Lord heal the hurt in your heart and replace the resentment you have felt for them, with love.

It is amazing how praying for the person and seeking to serve them can change your attitude towards them (see Matthew 5:44). A visit, a letter or a telephone call may be needed to put the relationship right. It may be painful to do so, but we have a choice of hurt pride or a ruined relationship.

> Therefore if you bring your gift to the altar, and there remember that your brother has something against you, leave your gift there before the altar, and go your way. First be reconciled to your brother, and then come and offer your gift.
>
> Matthew 5:23–24

17

Guilt

'And forgive us our debts, as we forgive our debtors. And do not lead us into temptation, but deliver us from the evil one'

King David was a 'man after God's own heart' (1 Samuel 13:14), someone who enjoyed a deep love relationship with the Lord and knew how to worship. But unfortunately he could also be said to be 'a man after his neighbour's wife'. Having committed adultery with the wife of one of his most faithful soldiers and having made her pregnant, he had the man killed to cover up his sin. It was not until God sent one of his prophets to confront David with his action that the king experienced true repentance. Consider how David must have felt before receiving God's forgiveness: 'When I kept silent, my bones grew old through my groaning all the day long, for day and night your hand was heavy upon me; my vitality was turned into the drought of summer' (Psalm 32:3–4).

Sin produces guilt and a fear of being found out. This, in turn, causes internal anguish and makes us uncomfortable in God's presence. The Psalmist went on to say, 'I acknowledged my sin to you, and my iniquity I have not hidden. I said, "I will confess my transgressions to the Lord," and you forgave the iniquity of my sin' (Psalm 32:5). 'Blessed is he whose transgression is forgiven, whose sin is covered. Blessed is the man to whom the Lord does not impute iniquity, and in whose spirit there is no guile' (Psalm 32:1–2).

God challenges us about our sin, not to condemn us, but so that we can experience his forgiveness. He wants us to be comfortable in his presence.

Comfortable in God's presence

The depth of God's love and forgiveness is beyond our comprehension. It is supernatural. It was while we were sinners that he loved us and Christ died for us (Romans 5:8). When we were naturally unlovable, God loved us. He saw us at our worst and said, 'I love you.' Why did God love us in this way? Because we were nice people? Because we were kind people? No, because love is his nature. He needed no ulterior motive. God chose to love us. He chose to die for our sin. Now he calls us to receive the love and forgiveness he offers.

In Jesus' parable of the prodigal son, we see something of what our heavenly father is like. On the return of his wayward son, who had misused his father and dragged his name into the dirt, we do not see a critical judgemental old man awaiting his son in order to bring a sound scolding, but one who 'When he was still a great way off...saw him and had compassion and ran and fell on his neck and kissed him' (Luke 15:20). He did not want to take his son back as a slave, to do penance for his sin, but accepted him back unreservedly as his child and fully restored him to sonship, telling his servants to remove the son's filthy rags, and place on him a clean robe, that the pollution from his past life be no more remembered. He gave him shoes to wear. Only sons wore shoes; slaves had bare feet. His father did not want a slave but a son! He gave him a ring, and had the fatted calf killed, saying, 'Let us eat and be merry; for this my son was dead and is alive again; he was lost and is found' (Luke 15:23–24).

We will never be comfortable in God's presence, until we realize that he is our father, one who loves and cares for us, one who offers us supernatural forgiveness. So often we stay in the far country, trying to prove that we are sorry, slavishly doing a servant's activities, hoping to earn favour. God invites us back as sons. When everything in us wants to hide, especially if we have committed the same sin again, and the words come from our lips, 'Lord, I've done it again', he still loves us and wants us to experience his forgiveness. This is not an excuse for sin, for a true recognition of God's love should cause us to hate doing those things which hurt him.

The words, 'Do not lead us into temptation, but deliver us from the evil one', remind us how dependent we are on the Lord to help us stand in victory. 'Forgive us' relates to the past; 'lead us' concerns the future. Although ultimately as Christians we sin by choice, he will 'keep us from stumbling' (Jude 24), if we will be kept (Jude 21)! Here, we are praying that the Lord will make us aware of temptations in advance, so that we are forewarned and thus forearmed. Also, we are asking that he will give us fresh strength daily, so that we may come out of each situation we face in victory.

Maybe as you read this, you are in a far country, like that prodigal son. Will you come back to God? Notice that the story is of the prodigal son, not the prodigal sinner. He was a son, who had backslidden. God loves you and wants you to experience his forgiveness. There are no surprises to God. Your actions do not catch him off guard. Even before he saved you, he knew what would happen, yet still he loved you.

It is 'In the time of need' that God invites us to 'Come boldly to the throne of grace, that we might obtain mercy' (Hebrews 4:16). Whilst there is guilt in our lives we cannot enjoy the Lord, nor the life of faith that he calls us to. A backslidden Christian is in a sorry state, he knows too much to enjoy the world fully, and yet misses out on the blessings of walking with God.

> There once was a prodigal son,
> Who said, 'Though I thought it was fun,
> To do what I like,
> Now I'll go on a hike,
> Home to Dad' and a new life begun.
>
> *M. Darwood*

God promises that 'If we confess our sins [that is, own up to them] he is faithful and just [there is no question about the matter] to forgive us our sins and to cleanse us from all unrighteousness' (1 John 1:9). When we confess our sin and own up to it, God is faithful and freely forgives. Many Christians grovel through life. God wants to forgive us so that we can lift our heads high as his sons, saved totally by his grace, and able to come boldly before him. Forgiveness is God's free gift, it is something we could never buy nor earn. He invites you to come and receive it—*right now*:

> Beloved, if our heart does not condemn us, we have confidence towards God. And whatever we ask we receive from him, because we keep his commandments and do those things that are pleasing in his sight.
>
> 1 John 3:21–22

18

Presumption

'For yours is the kingdom and the power and the glory for ever. Amen' (Matthew 6:13).

Because God answered our own or someone else's prayer in a certain way, it does not follow that he will do it the same way the next time. God has committed himself to meeting our needs, but he has not committed himself to the way that he will do it. It may be an unexpected gift in an envelope through the door. Many of us could testify to that happening. It may be the maturing of an insurance policy or legacy. It might be a product reduced in a shop. His answer might be, 'If any man will not work, let him not eat': a challenge to diligence. If we have not been faithful in all our giving, it might be the word, '"Bring all the tithes into the storehouse...and *prove me* now in this," says the Lord of Hosts, "If I will not...pour out for you such blessing that there will not be room enough to receive it"' (Malachi 3:10). If you don't sow, you won't reap! As you seek him, God will have just the right word for you.

Very rarely was the same miracle in the Bible repeated; God loves variety. Many healings are recorded, but each time God chose a new and fresh way of doing them. David prayed, 'Keep back your servant also from presumptuous sins' (Psalm 19:13). So many Christians confuse faith with presumption. One is godly, while the other is sinful. Some Christians stumble when they tell the Lord how to answer their prayer or base their expectations on what God did with someone else, so when he does not do it the way they expected him to, they are thrown. We read in John 6 that many of Jesus' disciples stumbled and backslid because of certain things he said: 'This is a hard saying; who can understand it?' (verse 60). His words did not fit in with their expectations or with their theological understanding. They had a set idea of what they expected God to do, so when he did it differently, it threw them. They were presumptuous.

On one occasion, I was travelling to preach at a church with a small team, but we ran out of petrol on the journey. We had about a hundred miles to go, including getting home again and there were no petrol stations open, so we prayed, 'Lord, if you want us there you are going to have to get us there and we trust you to get us home as well.' I said, 'Lord, I'm happy to sit here all day, but I believe you want us there, so I am going to turn the ignition, and start the car.' I turned the key, started the engine, drove to the meeting and on arrival back at my house, the car stopped in the entrance to the drive and rolled into its place! The next day I drove down to the garage in another car with a spare petrol can to get enough fuel to drive my car to the garage and fill the tank up.

That was a tremendous miracle. However, on another occasion I ran out of petrol and God's word to me was, 'Walk!' As I walked the two miles to the petrol station, with the spare can in my hand, I learned an important lesson: *you cannot take God for granted.*

Presumption is sin. When Jesus was tempted by the devil to jump off the mountain, the devil was tempting him to be presumptuous, but Jesus replied, 'You shall not tempt the Lord your God' (Matthew 4:7).

On one occasion, Jesus sent out his disciples on a mission saying, 'Carry neither purse, sack, nor sandals ... remain in the same house, eating and drinking such things as they give, for the labourer is worthy of his wages' (Luke 10:4–7). However, on another occasion he said to them, '"When I sent you without purse, sack, and sandals, did you lack anything?" So they said, "Nothing." Then he said to them, "But now, he who has a purse, let him take it, and likewise a sack"' (Luke 22:35–36).

Some Christians would say dogmatically that believers should never take a purse, sack, sandals—medication, life assurance, travel insurance, etc. Others would say, 'We must use our common sense and take our sack, sandals, purse, etc.' However, there is no hard and fast rule, God's direction may well be different on two similar occasions.

Such statements as, 'I never lock my car up; I trust the Lord', although they could be said in faith, are often the result of laziness, presumption or plain stupidity. If necessary, angels would have protected the Lord from harm, but Jesus made it clear that it was wrong to test God.

'Should I continue taking my medication now?'

'I'm travelling abroad, should I take out travel insurance?'

In answer to these questions, some Christians instantly respond with the statement, 'Where is your faith, brother? Trust God ' I believe that such things as medication, life insurance policies or travel insurance can be taken out in faith. They could be the provision of God. It was God who put the penicillin in the mould and gave men the ability to discover it. I believe that doctors are on the side of health, just as God is. I personally recommend that any ceasing of major medication should only be done with medical oversight. A miracle God performs is well able to stand up to any examination.

Many Christians put pressure on other believers to act presumptuously. Such decisions are between an individual and God. I dare not make them for you. Trying to prove our point or to impress others by our actions has, sadly, had some disastrous results in the past. I must discover God's will for me. Presumption acts to see 'if it works' and usually ends up disappointed. We cannot impress God.

PART THREE

Living by Faith

19

Living by Faith

Around 600 B.C. the prophet Habakkuk had a revelation from the Lord, one which we need today, that 'the just shall live by his faith'.

> Then the Lord answered me and said:
> 'Write the vision
> And make it plain on tablets
> That he may run who reads it.
> For the vision is yet for an appointed time;
> But at the end it will speak, and it will not lie.
> Though it tarries, wait for it;
> Because it will surely come,
> It will not tarry.
> Behold the proud,
> His soul is not upright in him;
> But the just shall live by his faith.'
>
> Habukkuk 2:2–4

It is exciting how the New Testament expands and enlarges what God has revealed to us in the Old Testament. In the books of Romans, Galatians and Hebrews that same scripture passage is taken and expanded.

In Romans 1 the emphasis is on the just, on the importance of a righteous lifestyle. We have considered how sin can hinder our seeing answered prayer. '"The just shall live by faith." For the wrath of God is revealed from heaven against all ungodliness and unrighteousness of men, who suppress the truth in unrighteousness' (Romans 1:17–18).

In Hebrews 10 and 11, the emphasis is on faith.

Then in Galatians 3:11 we read, 'That no one is justified by the law in the sight of God is evident, for "The just shall live by faith."' Here the emphasis is on living.

Paul's controversy at Galatia was with certain legalistic believers who were trying to bring the church back under the law, to living by rules and regulations. As Paul pointed out, 'God has redeemed us from the curse of the law' (Galatians 3:13). God wants us to enjoy life to the full.

Living by faith is not just for ministers and evangelists, but God's call for every Christian. When Jesus said, 'If you ask anything in my name, I will do it' (John 14:14), it was like giving us a signed cheque on the bank of heaven, then inviting us to fill in the details!

______ 19___

The Royal Bank of Father, Son and Holy Spirit Unlimited

Pay ______ or order

______ Jesus

Let us then consider a few areas of our inheritance, which we receive by faith.

1. We are saved by faith

'For by grace you have been saved through faith, and that not of yourselves; it is the gift of God, not of works, lest anyone should boast' (Ephesians 2:8–9).

'A man is justified by faith apart from the deeds of the law' (Romans 3:28).

We cannot save ourselves, nor is there anything we can do to earn our salvation. It is God's free gift to us.

'If you confess with your mouth the Lord Jesus and believe in your heart that God has raised him from the dead, you will be saved. For with the heart one believes to righteousness, and with the mouth confession is made to salvation' (Romans 10:9).

Many people have no assurance that they are saved until they have actually confessed the fact. When I lead people to the Lord, I encourage them to tell someone else what has happened, to put into their own words what has taken place. It seals something inside.

Jesus came that we might know that we have eternal life. He said, 'Most assuredly, I say to you, he who hears my words and believes in him who sent me *has* eternal life and *shall not* come into judgement, but has passed from death into life' (John 5:24).

Have you heard his words and believed in him? If so, then you have eternal life! Eternal life does not begin when we die, it begins now. It is eternal, because it never finishes.

2. Empowered by the Holy Spirit by faith

Paul asked the Galatian church, 'Did you receive the Spirit by works of the law or by hearing of faith...

Therefore he who supplies the Spirit to you and works miracles among you, does he do it by works of the law, or by the hearing of faith?' (Galatians 3:2, 5).

We receive the empowering of the Holy Spirit by faith and there is nothing to fear.

> If a son asks for bread from any father among you, will he give him a stone? Or if he asks for a fish, will he give him a serpent instead of a fish? Or if he asks for an egg, will he offer him a scorpion? If you then, being evil, know how to give good gifts to your children, how much more will your heavenly Father give the Holy Spirit to those who ask him!'
>
> Luke 11:11–13

Again, God promises that all we have to do is ask and we will receive.

3. We walk victoriously by faith

> For whoever is born of God overcomes the world. And this is the victory that has overcome the world—our faith.
>
> 1 John 5:4

> Therefore do not let sin reign in your mortal body, that you should obey it in its lusts. And do not present your members as instruments of unrighteousness to sin, but present yourselves to God as being alive from the dead, and your members as instruments of righteousness to God. For sin shall not have dominion over you, for you are not under law but under grace.
>
> Romans 6:12–14

Do not blame the devil when you sin. Do not say, 'I couldn't help it.' God says that you can! The Christian sins by choice. God will not allow us to be tempted above the point where we are able to stand victorious (1 Corinthians 10:13). We can live victoriously if we are willing to say, as Jesus did, 'Not my will but your will be done.' So, above all, take 'the *shield of faith* with which you will be able to quench *all* the fiery darts of the wicked one' (Ephesians 6:16).

4. We receive healing by faith

> When evening had come, they brought to him many who were demon-possessed. And he cast out the spirits with a word and healed all who were sick, that it might be fulfilled which was spoken by Isaiah the prophet, saying: 'He himself took our infirmities and bore our sickness.'
>
> Matthew 8:16–17

We have seen that all who came to Jesus in faith received healing. God desires that we be as physically well as we are spiritually (3 John 2) and promises that 'The prayer of faith will save the sick, and the Lord will raise him up. And if he has committed sins he will be forgiven' (James 5:15).

'Bless the Lord, O my soul, and forget not all his benefits: who forgives *all* your iniquities, who heals *all* your diseases' (Psalm 103:2–3).

5. We receive material provision by faith

'My God shall supply all your need according to his riches in glory by Christ Jesus' (Philippians 4:19). Where does God's supply for our needs come from? Out of his riches in glory. His resources are inexhaustible!

> Therefore I say to you, do not worry about your life, what you will eat or what you will drink; nor about your

> body, what you will put on. Is not life more than food and the body more than clothing? Look at the birds of the air, for they neither sow nor reap nor gather into barns; yet your heavenly Father feeds them. Are you not of more value than they?...But seek first the kingdom of God and his righteousness, and all these things shall be added to you.
>
> Matthew 6:25–26, 33

As we saw in chapter 15, many Christians have exalted poverty, as though it were a godly thing. God hates poverty! What reflection is it on his Fatherhood if his children are living in poverty? In the Bible financial prosperity is linked with such things as godliness and giving (Proverbs 13:22; Psalm 37:25).

> He who sows sparingly will also reap sparingly, and he who sows bountifully will also reap bountifully. So let each one give as he purposes in his heart, not grudgingly or of necessity; for God loves a cheerful giver. And God is able to make all grace abound towards you, that you, always having all sufficiency in all things, may have an abundance for every good work.
>
> 2 Corinthians 9:6–8

God does not prosper us so that we can hoard, but so that all our needs can be met and we still have more to give away to bless others. If we hoard, our supply will run out, but if we give, God will give back.

6. We receive freedom from fear and anxiety by faith

'God has not given us a spirit of fear, but of power and of love and of a sound mind' (2 Timothy 1:7). So if there are fears in your life, guess where they come from? Fear robs us of a sound mind, but Jesus came to set us free. It is possible to live free from fear. One key is to realize that Jesus really is on the throne. He is in control and he will never leave you nor forsake you.

One day as the disciples were out in a boat, a storm broke out. In fear, the disciples cried out, 'Lord, save us! We are perishing!' So Jesus rebuked the storm and the wind and there was a great calm. Now in your situation, hear Jesus' voice speaking, 'Peace, be still.' Let him calm the storm that you are experiencing (Matthew 8:23–27).

David said, 'I sought the Lord, and he heard me, and delivered me from all my fears' (Psalm 34:4). And all means all, including *any* you may have!

7. We eat by faith

We are even called to 'eat from faith' (Romans 14:23). The apostle Paul warned Timothy against those who had departed from the faith:

> Commanding to abstain from foods which God created to be received with thanksgiving by those who believe and know the truth. For every creature of God is good, and nothing is to be refused if it is received with thanksgiving; for it is sanctified by the word of God and prayer.
>
> 1 Timothy 4:3–5

I do not say grace as a religious ritual, but I do pray that God will sanctify the food and kill any harmful germs. Having my food sanctified is important, especially in view of some of the things I have had set before me in foreign countries!

8. Ultimately, we can die by faith

Not only are we called to live by faith; in the book of

Hebrews we read of some who died by faith (Hebrews 11:35–40).

For the Christian death is not defeat. On earth we can experience a foretaste of the health we will experience in heaven. We can have a foretaste of God's provision when our needs are met. However, in heaven there will be no sickness and no needs. One day, unless Christ returns first, we are all going to die. Are you ready? Are you sure of Christ's forgiveness?

For the saint, to be absent from the body is to be present with the Lord (2 Corinthians 5:8). The apostle Paul said:

> For to me, to live is Christ, and *to die is gain*. But if I live on in the flesh, this will mean fruit from my labour; yet what I shall choose I cannot tell. For I am hard pressed between the two, having a desire to depart and be with Christ, which is far better. Nevertheless to remain in the flesh is more needful for you.
>
> Philippians 1:21–24

Why was death gain for Paul? Because he knew where he was going: straight into the full presence of God.

When David Watson was interviewed on the radio a short while before his death, Nick Page asked him, 'What happens if you find that healing is not coming?'

David wisely replied, 'If I found it was not coming, I hope I have got to the position of really trusting in Christ that the best is yet to be. You know, actually to be with Christ and free for ever from the pain and suffering, tears and problems and injustices of this world there is nothing more glorious than that. That is why I genuinely am at the place where I really want to be in heaven (sometimes the sooner, the better), but I am willing to be on this earth, with all its struggles and battles if he wants me here.'

Ultimately, God does not guarantee us immunity from death, but he does promise us eternity in his presence, which nothing can rob us of.

In our dear brother David Watson's case, our loss was heaven's gain. 'Precious in the sight of the Lord is the death of his saints' (Psalm 116:15). For the saint, death is not defeat or a threat, but ultimate healing!

One day we will go to be with Christ, but, until then, we have an exciting walk of faith ahead—*enjoy it*!

Appendix

In closing, here are sixteen questions I am frequently asked relating to the whole area of faith, with references back to relevant passages in the book.

1. Isn't it selfish to expect our prayers to be answered? 123–130
2. Is faith really important in seeing our prayers answered? 18–19, 29–30, 51–59
3. Won't events happen whether or not we pray? 13–17, 61–64
4. Why are we not seeing a greater breakthrough of the miraculous in our land? 43–50
5. How do I get rid of my unbelief? 43–47
6. How do I get more faith? 35–42, 52–53
7. Is hope different from faith? 54–55
8. How do I discover God's will in areas like healing? 23–33
9. Is the use of medication or insurance a lack of faith? 143–146
10. I've been prayed for to be healed, but I appear to be no different. What can I do? 72, 75–87
11. Can I be prayed for again? 79
12. Can wrong attitudes stop our prayers being answered? 105–107, 124–128
13. I've been prayed for to be healed. Should I now stop taking my medication? 145–146
14. I've sinned. Will God forgive me? 137–141
15. Even after prayer, they died. Why? 155–157
16. Why does God allow trials? 89–101